Seven Plays by Argentine Playwright Susana Torres Molina (*Strange Toy, That's All That, Mystic Union, Sirens' Song, Paradises Lost, Zero,* and *She*)

Susana Torres Molina

SEVEN PLAYS BY ARGENTINE PLAYWRIGHT SUSANA TORRES MOLINA (*STRANGE TOY, THAT'S ALL THAT, MYSTIC UNION, SIRENS' SONG, PARADISES LOST, ZERO,* AND *SHE*)

Edited, with an Introduction, by
María Claudia André

Translated from Spanish into English by
María Claudia André and Barbara Younoszai

The Edwin Mellen Press
Lewiston•Queenston•Lampeter

Library of Congress Cataloging-in-Publication Data

Molina, Susana Torres
 Seven plays by Argentine playwright Susana Torres Molina (Strange Toy, That's All That, Mystic Union, Sirens' Song, Paradises Lost, Zero, and She)
/ edited, with an introduction, by María Claudia André ; translated from Spanish into English by María Claudia André and Barbara Younoszai.
    p. cm.
 Includes bibliographical references.
 ISBN-13: 978-0-7734-5620-4
 ISBN-10: 0-7734-5620-1
 I. Title.

hors série.

A CIP catalog record for this book is available from the British Library.

Copyright © 2006 María Claudia André

All rights reserved. For information contact

> The Edwin Mellen Press
> Box 450
> Lewiston, New York
> USA 14092-0450

> The Edwin Mellen Press
> Box 67
> Queenston, Ontario
> CANADA L0S 1L0

> The Edwin Mellen Press, Ltd.
> Lampeter, Ceredigion, Wales
> UNITED KINGDOM SA48 8LT

Printed in the United States of America

Table of Contents

Preface by Jean Graham-Jones / i

Acknowledgements / iii

Introduction / 1

Interview with Susana Torres Molina / 13

Strange Toy (*Extraño juguete*) / 21

That's All That (*...y a otra cosa mariposa*) / 73

Mystic Union (*Mystic unio*) / 121

Sirens' Song (*Canto de sirenas*) / 156

Paradises Lost (*Paraísos Perdidos*) / 168

Zero (*Cero*) / 183

She (*Ella*) / 199

Bibliography / 226

Preface

Susana Torres Molina is an artist of "firsts." From her 1982 *Dueña y señora*, the first collection of openly erotic short stories by a Latin American woman writer, to the 1991 *Unió mystica*, the first Argentinean play about AIDS, to her innovative Butoh-inspired stagings, Torres Molina has valiantly marched into the unknown in a country that takes frequent refuge in the known–in its prescribed modes of gendered behavior, in its Manichean national self-image, and even in its limited and often compartmentalized performance aesthetics. Torres Molina's plays have questioned all of these comfortable assumptions.

It should therefore not surprise the readers of this collection to learn that Torres Molina's is a theatre of paradox and tension, but it might startle them to find out that it is also a theatre of great humor and aesthetic beauty. Beginning with her first play, the 1977 *Extraño juguete* [Strange Toy], Torres Molina's theatre has based itself on the rules of a droll but serious game of mediation, in which all construction is foregrounded. Plays as 1981's highly regarded *...y a otra cosa mariposa* [That's All That], in which all four male characters are mediated through female actors, point to a flexible and thus transformative attitude toward sociosexual roles. Nevertheless, for a playwright often aligned with a humorously critical feminist perspective, recent plays such as *Lo que no se nombra* [The Unnamable] and *Ella* [She] offer exclusively male characters in cruelly tragic circumstances.

It may seem additionally strange that a playwright, director and scenographer such as Torres Molina, whose work has most often been associated with the so-called "theatre of image," now presents us with a collection of plays, whose very written nature privileges word over image. It is further telling that her most "experiential" and aesthetically sublime play, the 1988 *Amantissima*, is not found in this collection. Nevertheless, as the reader will soon see, Torres Molina's dialogues crackle with a witty and concise lyricism.

Susana Torres Molina has not created these plays in isolation. On the contrary, collaboration has been key to her development as a writer and theater practitioner. Torres Molina has written collectively, creating with others such plays as 1983's *Inventario* [Inventory]. She has worked transatlantically, producing the monologue *Nada entre los dientes* [Nothing Between the Teeth] and *Lo que no se nombra* (the result of an exercise in creating a play from a newspaper headline published on the day of the author's birth) out of ongoing conversations between Spanish and Argentinean playwrights. And of course she has worked locally as a jury member for *Teatroxlaidentidad* 2001 [Theatreforidentity 2001] festival of forty-one one-act plays focused around the ongoing work of the grandmothers of the children of the disappeared as they seek to account for the some five hundred children still missing. Unsurprisingly, Torres Molina often speaks of the importance of the "group" (witnessed in the interview included in this collection) and attributes her most recent creations to her weekly meetings with four other Buenos Aires playwrights.

The result of all this creative activity is a collection of plays whose translation into English is long overdue. The collected works take some of their inspiration from the author's immediate lived experiences, but, with the able assistance of translators María Claudia André and Barbara Younousai (Strange Toy) they easily make the linguistic and cultural move to the English-speaking stage. Susana Torres Molina speaks, not to some imagined universal reader-spectator, but to a contemporary audience living fully in a global community whose colonial, imperial and patriarchal roots are still showing.

Jean Graham-Jones - Florida State University

Acknowledgements

I wish to thank Susana Torres Molina not only for granting me the honor to translate her works, but also for her unwavering support, her collaboration, and her friendship. I would like to extend my deepest gratitude to Jane Brodey, Jean Graham-Jones, Priscilla Atkins, and Tabitha Miller for their insightful comments and corrections. Their genuine commitment and dedication contributed to the successful completion of this project.

Introduction

This anthology features a selection of translated plays by Argentine actress and playwright Susana Torres Molina. The seven pieces gathered in this collection are some of the works that established Torres Molina's reputation as one of the most outstanding and innovative female playwrights in contemporary Latin American theatre. *Strange Toy, That's All That,* and *She* all are winners of prestigious national and international awards, and have received the recognition of fellow dramatists and literary critics in the academic circle. Each piece not only reveals the author's creative talents as dramatist, director, and stage designer, but also offers an aesthetic perspective that challenges more realistic and conventional forms of playwriting.

Apart from serving as a literary outlet for the works of an accomplished and internationally acclaimed female author, this collection intends to introduce English-speaking audiences to the styles and techniques developed by contemporary Argentine playwrights, and to further deepen the appreciation of those already familiar with it. In order to satisfy the interests of scholars, dramatists and theatre audiences alike, only those pieces that combine a high aesthetic quality and feasible playability were considered for publication. Finally, so as to enhance the reader's appreciation of Torres Molina's evolution as a dramatist, the plays are presented in the chronological order in which they were written. Each piece is introduced by a brief outline indicating the place, the year of performance and the awards received.

About the author:

Susana Torres Molina (Buenos Aires, 1946) is an accomplished playwright, director, and actress whose unparalleled approach to drama has significantly expanded the margins of Latin American theater. She began her theater career as an actress, participating in plays such as *Libertad y otras intoxicaciones* (1967) [Freedom and other intoxications] and *Señor Frankenstein* (1968) [Mister Frankenstein], productions sponsored by the enormously influential Di Tella Institute. She also had the opportunity to work with important directors Beatriz Matar, in *El baño de los pájaros* (1977) [Bird's Bath], and Laura Yussem, in *Boda blanca* (1981) [White Wedding].

In 1981, she received the first prize in the Primer Encuentro de Teatro Joven (Buenos Aires, 1981) for her play *Extraño juguete* (1977) [Strange Toy]; in 1980, her short films *Pettoruti* and *Lina y Tina* were respectively awarded the First Prize by Fondo Nacional de las Artes and the International Short Film Festival in Huesta, Spain. In 1978, under the dictatorial regime in Argentina, Torres Molina, her (ex)husband --playwright and actor Eduardo Pavlovsky-- and their three children exiled to Madrid, where they resided until 1981. While in Spain, she worked as an actress and restaged *Extraño juguete* under the direction of renowned actress Norma Aleandro.

Some of her recent works as a writer and director include: *Soles* (1982) [Suns]; *Inventario* (1983) [Inventory] co-written with Carlos Somigliana, Hebe Serebrinsky and Peñarol Méndez for Teatro Abierto's third annual festival[1]; *Espiral de fuego* (1985) [Spiral of Fire]; *Amantíssima* (1988) [Beloved]; *Unió Mystica* (1991) [Mystic Unio]; *...y a otra cosa mariposa* (1981) [That's All That] read at the 3rd. International Women Playwrights Conference in Adelaide, Australia; *Canto de sirenas* (1995) [Sirens' Song]; *Ensayo* (monologue for the multiple award winning show *A corazón abierto*, (1996) [Essay]; *Paraísos perdidos* (1997) [Paradises Lost]; *Manifiesto* (unstaged, 1998) [Manifest]; *No sé* *tú* (1999) [Maybe You]; *Nada entre los dientes* (monologue, 1999) [Nothing Between the Teeth]; *Cero* (1999) [Zero]; *Hormigas en el bidet* (1999) [Ants in the Bidet]; *Una noche cualquiera* (unstaged, 1999) [Any other night], recipient of the XVIII Theatre Award "Hermanos Machado" in Seville, Spain; *Lo que no se nombra* (2000) [The Unnamable], winner of the IV Concurso Nacional de Obras Breves in 2001, and *Ella* (2001) [She], first prize winner of the Concurso de Obras Teatrales del Fondo Nacional de las Artes. Most recently, Torres Molina has collaborated with directors Daniel Marcove and Rubén Pires in *Como si nada* (2000) [As if nothing], piece performed in *La mayor, la menor y el del medio* [The Oldest, The Youngest and The One in the Middle], and in *Sorteo* [Raffle], staged at the 2001 Teatroxlaidentidad Festival [Theatre for Identity]. Also staged in 2001 were *Fría como azulejo de cocina*, [Cold as Kitchen Tile], directed by Antonio Celico, a production based on selections from *Dueña y Señora*, (short stories, 1982) [Mistress and Lady], and *Azul Metalizado* [Metallic Blue], directed by Guillermo Guío. Moreover, in 2002, Torres Molina staged and directed *Serie: Actos privados* [Series: Private Acts], a three-play show featuring *Nada entre los dientes* (1999), *Turning Point* (2002), and *Modus operandi* (2002). *Estática* (2002) [Static] was a finalist for the "Casa de America" award.

In addition to writing, directing, and participating in all forms of theatre production, Torres Molina has authored television, film, dance scripts, and collaborated with renowned musicians and singers. In 1999, she conducted creative research workshops with HIV-positive inmates from the Devoto penitentiary, and in 2002 she worked with doctors from the Hospital Alvarez. Her plays have been performed in New York, Washington DC, Río de Janeiro, Madrid, London, Mexico City and Montevideo.

Themes and Techniques:

Torres Molina's cutting-edge dramaturgy is an explosive combination of sarcasm and reflective critique, an introspective game of hide-and-seek, an invitation to both redefine and question the limits of individuality outside the parameters of conventionalisms. Breaking away from traditional forms of theatrical discourse, her work offers a unique perspective of the emotional and psychological complexity of the human existence. Metaphysical anxiety, the absurdity of the human condition, and man's alienation in modern society are some of the current themes on her dramaturgy. Her plays, however, transmit a passion for life with all the risks and challenges that it has to offer.

Torres Molina's distinctive interpretation of reality and poignant sense of humor are representative of a generation of Argentine women playwrights --like Diana Raznovich and Cristina Escofet-- interested in the deconstruction of prescribed gender roles and masculine hierarchies that perpetuate gender based stereotypes. Her first plays, *Strange Toy* and *That's All That* are perfect examples of such a vision. As Jacqueline Bixler examines, "In both pieces, Torres Molina relies on framed role playing to provide new, dominant roles for women, roles that she has purloined from the masculine repertoire--employer, exploiter, harasser, macho, to name just a few" (216).[2]

Strange Toy, masterfully translated by Barbara Younoszai,[3] is a game-structured play in which two middle-aged spinsters, Perla and Angélica, receive the unexpected visit of a lingerie salesman. Role-playing and the erotic playfulness of the dialogue lead to the sexual arousal of the sadomasochist vendor, who seems to enjoy the spinsters' physical and emotional abuse. As the play unfolds, the dynamics of the game intensify, climaxing in a scene in which the man interrupts his performance to relieve himself. It is only at this point that the viewer realizes all has been a charade prearranged by the two well-off, bored matrons in search of a thrill. In this metatheatrical piece, Torres Molina not only renders a poignant critique of the overwhelming repressive conditions imposed by Argentina's dictatorial regime, but also exposes the manipulative ploys of the upper class willing to pay for their own enjoyment. Frustration, anger, fear, irony, and a heavy dose of sarcasm are the main elements of this theatrical game in which emotions and feelings are manipulated for the thrill of an affluent consumer. As Denise Di Puccio examines, "Completely divested of control over their emotional lives, these rich women cannot feel happiness or sadness unless they pay for it. A virtual emotional buffet of mental states (including happiness, sadness, terror, sexuality, maternity, anger, boredom, and exhaustion), is laid bare for purchase and consumption by the two sisters"(157).[4] Transforming every discourse of power into an irreverent parody, the playwright raises the spectators' awareness on the consumerist vein of modern culture, while simultaneously reflects upon the perpetual acting and role-playing required to fulfill societal expectations within our own daily routine. According to Catherine Larson, contemporary Latin American women dramatists' use of literal or metaphoric game-playing and role-playing function as self-conscious techniques that defy patriarchal structures of dominance (78).[5] By reinventing the rules of the game in their own terms, women are able to defy, through symbolic representation, "the violence and torture that occur on a political level" as well as "the domestic interactions that take place within the family unit"(83).

In *That's All That*, Torres Molina challenges institutionalized categorizations of sex and gender by focusing on the behavior, language and dynamics of four *porteño* [people from Buenos Aires], male friends through the span of a lifetime. Interestingly, in this *tour de force* script, the roles of El Flaco [Skinny], El Inglés [The Brit], Cerdín [Fatso] and Pajarito [Finch], must be strictly performed by women dressed in men's clothing. Indeed, as Jean Graham-Jones indicates, "The reading, and appreciation, of this play lies in the fact that both sexes are present throughout the performance, thus providing a constant humanization to counter the dehumanizing process of sexist mythologizing"(100).[6] Through a witty and sarcastic dialogue heavily influenced by *porteño* slang and mannerisms that best capture the characteristic demeanor of the Argentine male, the dramatist underscores the performance quality of gender as a social construct.

Significant to the playwright's discourse is the representation of the body as an instrument with which to subvert the patriarchal prescriptions of gender. Set as a paradigm of resistance, the body becomes a repository to recycle postmodern constructs of beauty, sexuality, eroticism and power. For Graham-Jones, the powerful impression created by the four women playing the males roles creates a distancing effect that alienates the text from its actors, thus forcing the spectator to re-evaluate not only the plays' content, but also the actors' performance. Graham-Jones points out that "each time Woman is objectified and thus dehumanized in the text, this would-be dehumanization is counteracted by the very physical human presence of the women portraying these characters, their social condition as women reinforced and even exaggerated by costuming and makeup"(100).

Embarked upon a metaphysical quest, Torres Molina's characters frequently move behind light into the shadows of the unconscious in search of their true self. To reach the deepest stratum of individuality, her subjects are frequently devoid of name and presented in the typical role of the Father, the Mother, the Wife, or simply as He or She. Such ambiguity not only expands the narrow configuration of a single character into multiple alternatives, but it also serves as a powerful means to explore the psychological traits and motivations characteristic of the gender roles socially assigned.

Since the '80s, Torres Molina's theatrical discourse has shifted from the European and the Argentine tradition developing into a more personal and unique style. As the dramatist herself acknowledges, some of her influences come from the image-based spectacle of Butô or Butoh (The Dance of Shadows)[7], a particular form of contemporary Japanese dance that challenges the classic and more traditional Western influences. This expressionist technique involves music, movement, and repeated or symbolic actions performed by characters in white make-up and almost naked bodies.

Beloved is a visually stunning piece that moves away from the conventions of dramatic speech to follow "a theatrical trend known as 'teatro de imágenes' [theater of images], in which strong, expressionistic images and metaphor take precedence over conventional, causal structure and dialogue"(Bixler 216).[8] Stage devices, costumes, and lighting design are integrated to create an intense spectacle in which the language of the body predominates over the dramatic text. With *Beloved*, Torres Molina sets the pace for a more self-reflective and insightful dramatic text, one in which archetypal voices acquire the corporeal physicality of bodies, though never reaching the individuality of a fully developed character. Detached from a unanimous meaning, the poetic image regains its expressive freedom, thus enhancing the lyrical as well as the visual language of the play. *Beloved*, according to Bixler, displays "a clear progression toward a more feminist approach in both content and technique," and unlike her earlier work, this "is a woman's play from beginning to end--it is a play by women, about women and expressly for women"(217).

Mystic Unio also ascribes to such a theatrical style and technique by further exploring the ritualistic and the cyclic nature of the feminine self. Its theme, however, revolves around the feelings of anger, sadness and anguish of three women--the wife, the prostitute, and the lover--who have contracted HIV. According to the author, "the title identifies the mysterious union between sexual energy, mind, heart and body. Each of the characters represents one of these concepts. The woman is the mind, the ego, the selfish possessive aspect of love. The lover is the heart: unconditional love as an expression of an internal state that is, by nature, overwhelming. The prostitute, the instinct, the physical beyond the realm of the feelings."[9] The confessional tone of the play brings forth the intimacies of a feminine collective, whose secret desires and expectations will never be fulfilled. By confronting their fears of death or infection, these women desperately seek to find meaning behind their own existence, each one revealing different levels of frustration, anger, and passion. A disquieting trip through the empire of the senses, *Mystic Unio* guides the spectator to the core of the human soul, exposing its thirst for eternity and true communion.

Sirens' Song is a four-part "monologue-poem" in which physical movement, sound, and staging are masterfully combined to enhance the enigmatic quality of the text. Within the realm of a limbic region, we witness the formative experience of a creature half-women, half-animal that seeks the perfection of divinity. As the incarnation of Humanity, this mythical being wanders through the paths of Desire, Loneliness, Senses, and Passion, intending to liberate the mundane aspects of the soul. The enlightenment process brings her to the realization that love and compassion are the only gateways toward wisdom, spirituality and transcendence. Mirroring the aesthetics and the elucidation of religious texts like the Bible or the teachings of Buddha, the language of this parabolic play conveys a profound message of solidarity among human beings. As Jorge Dubatti explains, "Torres Molina continues, with variants that are proper of her self, the 'sacred theatre' project developed by Antonín Artaud in *The Theatre and Its Double* and by Peter Brook in *The Empty Space*, intertwining her ideas with threads of Oriental wisdom"(2).[10]

Paradises Lost is yet another powerful allegory of the existential quest and the sense of fulfillment. This highly engaging text focus on the intense dynamics between a man and a woman at the point of breaking up. Regret, anguish, and remorse are the wounds left after an intense relationship that, through the years, have endured the capricious and often contradictory rulings of the human heart.

Behind the crude realism sustained with peaks of dramatic tension, the emotionally charged dialogue constructs an intense atmosphere that renders a singular close-up of the couples' emotional disintegration. Charged with a heavy dose of irony and humor, *Paradises Lost* renders a clear reflection on the irrationality and compulsion of relationships based on passion. Opposite sides of the coin, love and hate, here stand, but a bexat apart, as a constant reminder of the paradoxical essence of the human experience.

Also in 1999, Torres Molina wrote *Zero* and *Hormigas en el bidet*, both directed by Ricardo Holcer and performed as part of a *Combinatoria de 8 en base 4* [Eight Combined Over a Base of Four], a show of eight one-act plays co-written with Patricia Zangaro, Javier Daulte, and Alfredo Megua. In *Zero*, as in *That's All That*, role-playing once again functions as an effective means to expose the performance quality of gender. Endorsing Judith Butler's argument that "gender is an 'act,' broadly construed, which constructs the social fiction of its own psychological interiority"(27-82),[11] this erotically charged play depicts a scenario in which the male body--instead of the female--becomes the icon of sexual objectification and physical submission. The piece illustrates, like an impressionist tableau, how sexual desire and possession are not exclusive to the male, but phenomenon pertinent to both sexes. As such, the drama renders an alternative that defies all gender demarcations by portraying women as clients and men as subjects of sexual exchange. In this scenario, eroticism and sexual pleasure become a commodity and consolation for those who are either afraid of losing control of their emotions. In *Zero*, sex-for-hire is both an alternative to avoid the pain of abandonment and a source of anticipated gratification, as planning, imagining and desiring are part of the service offered to satisfy consumers' needs.

With *She*, Torres Molina reverts to a more traditional dramatic discourse. This eleven-scene piece presents the conflict between two men who find themselves trapped by their feelings of love and lust for the same woman. Through situations that oscillate from the real to the absurd, the plot discloses the pathetic ploys of a man who psychologically manipulates his wife's lover as he seeks to match his own masculinity against that of his rival. SHE is a powerful character that never appears on stage; however, she is a key figure in the play. In this award-winning play in which nothing is what it seems, dramatic and humorous overtones combine to depict how the affliction and the fear of loneliness may trigger the cowardice and the cruelty of individuals consumed by the intensity of their own passions.

Torres Molina's literary corpus focuses on the human condition, exploring the deepest roots of the psychological and emotional conflicts that are inherent to society as a whole. Her constant experimentation with diverse forms of artistic expression make her an exceptional and a visionary playwright whose creative talent makes of the dramatic experience a cathartic practice to live out the daily contradictions and conflicts of being alive.

Notes

[1] Teatro Abierto (1983) [Open Theatre], as Graham-Jones explains, was a collective as well as an experimental theatre cycle which staged the works of seven groups, "each group comprised four playwrights and four directors, who then invited actors and technicians to participate" (97). The proposed theme for these groups was the expression and vision of what have happened during the last seven years under dictatorship in Argentina. See Jean Graham-Jones *Exorcising History Argentine Theatre under Dictatorship* (Lewisburg: Bucknell University Press, 2000).

[2] In *Latin American Women Dramatists: Theater, Texts and Theories*. Catherine Larson and Margarita Vargas, eds. (Bloomington: Indiana University Press, 1998).

[3] Barbara Younoszai completed her B.A., M.A. at UC Berkeley and her Ph.D. at the University of Minnesota. She is currently a professor at Hamline University, St. Paul, MN.

[4] In Denise DiPuccio's, "Radical and Materialist Relationships in Torres Molina's *Extraño juguete." Letras Femeninas* 21.1-2 (1995 Spring-Fall): 153-64

[5] In Larson's, *Latin American Women Dramatists: Theater, Texts and Theories*, 1998.

[6] See Jean Graham Jones, "Myths, Masks and Machismo: *Un trabajo fabuloso* by Ricardo Halalc and ...*Y a otra cosa mariposa* by Susana Torres Molina." *Gestos: Teoría y práctica del teatro hispánico*. 10-20 (Nov. 1995): 91-106.

[7] In 1998, Torres Molina directed *Tango Butoh* with Gustavo Collini Santor and participated in the Butoh Dance Festival in San Francisco, USA and Vancouver, Canada.

[8] Consult Jacqueline Bixler's, "For Women Only? The Theater of Susana Torres Molina." Larson's *In Latin American Women Dramatists: Theater, Texts, and Theories*, 1998. 215-33.

[9] Personal correspondence dated March 24, 2003.

[10] Susana Torres Molina, *Espiral de fuego/ Canto de sirenas* (Buenos Aires: Teatro Vivo, 2002).

[11] Consult Judith Butler, "Performative Acts and Gender Constitution: An Essay in Phenomenology and Feminist Theory." *Performing Feminisms.* Sue-Ellen Case, ed. (Baltimore: Johns Hopkins UP, 1990): 270-82.

Interview with Susana Torres Molina

MCA: When did you become a writer?

STM: Literature has always been my means of expression. At first, I wrote short stories, poetry, and my personal diary. Years later, when I began to study theatre to become an actress, I realized that it was very easy for me to write skits and scenes. My interest in drama sparked then, and the fact that I studied acting helped. In my texts, the theatrical is as important as the literary discourse. There is a marked difference when the piece is written departing from literature than when it is written departing from the body that performs it. I continued writing short stories and scripts for short films, cinema, and some for television. After a while, I started exploring different fields, and I believe that if I had stayed in Spain – where I had been living from 1978 to 1981– I would have probably pursued cinema, because that was what I was studying at the time. I did a short film that won three awards in international festivals: one in Huesca, another one in Valladolid, and a third award for the best short film of 1980 from the Spanish Ministry of Culture. Part of the winning prize constituted a grant to continue filmmaking; however, it was then that we all decided to return to Argentina, and ironically, upon my arrival I found out I had won the awards.

Once back home in Buenos Aires, cinematography seemed a very hard path to follow, while theatre was much more accessible, particularly at the level of production. I remember rehearsing some pieces in my own living room and selling the tickets ahead of time in order to be able to produce the play with that same cash. Financial interests are less conditioned in this medium since theatre is still a minority art form. I had already done some acting in Spain and performed in my own play *Extraño juguete* [Strange Toy, 1977]. I worked under Norma Aleandro's direction along with Tato Pavlovsky and Zulema Katz. Before exile, I had the leading role in *El baño de los pájaros* (Birdbath, 1977), a play by the U.S. writer Leonard Melfi, directed by Beatriz Matar. In 1981, I wrote and directed *...y a otra cosa mariposa* (That's All That, 1981). I wanted this play to be directed by a woman, however, at the time there were not many women directors, so I directed it myself. I stopped acting to take the role of the director. Lately, I work less as a director as I see myself more inclined toward the world of writing, a world that has an advantage in these chaotic and uncertain times when it is best not to depend on anything, save one's own dedication. In fact, I have increased the rhythm of my dramatic production since joining a self-study group with four other playwrights. Our meetings provide a space of exchange, stimulation, and reflection. I consider these meetings to be a great privilege and a continual source of creation.

MCA: How did you continue to evolve in reading and writing?

STM: I have always been an avid reader. During my childhood, I read the same literature that my older sister read. Most of the books were by classic or traditional authors such as Emilio Salgari, Agatha Christie, Chesterton, Poe... I also enjoyed reading detective stories and thrillers. At the age of fifteen, I became a fan of Herman Hesse, then I read *Steppenwolf, Demian,* and several of his novels. Later on, I continued with Rimbaud, Baudelaire, Michaux, Lautremont; and, of course, I read Argentine literature, such as Roberto Arlt, Leopoldo Marechal, Borges, Silvina Ocampo, Alejandra Pizarnik, and Olga Orozco.

MCA: Did your parents have any influence on your artistic career?

STM: No. I am the only one in the family with a passion for the arts in general and for literature in particular. The theatre was a place of easy access, but I have never thought theatre was my life and my only passion since I could be doing cinema or photography. Many different fields interest me. Still, the access to that discipline was something fluid, a possibility to express my imaginary world. A world that I have tried to represent in different ways through drama and scenic language, creating shows focused on visual effects, dance, and poetry. Sometimes I have been criticized for such experimentation because some critics do not consider it to be "theatre." The recent success of new performance trends has made their criteria a bit more flexible. For me, everything is a topic for personal investigation, and the artistic expression is a means to explore my own individuality. In this search, I became very interested in theatre-dance as well as in Butoh or *The Dance of the Shadows*, which is Japanese contemporary dance that challenges the classic and more traditional Western influences. It is a very expressive technique, strong and moving. The naked –or almost naked– body is totally made up in white, and the performers move like beings that are beyond life and death. *Amantissima* (1988) is a result of such influence and experimentation.

For more than fifteen years, I have coordinated workshops in creative research. These are workshops exclusively designed for people who are interested in investigating and developing their own creative potential. As I have always been naturally attracted to music, theatre, cinematography, literature, performance, and photography, the idea of creating workshops in which people would connect with their own possibilities through different means or different disciplines of expression was very exciting. My workshop is a place where people create and perform their own works. For example, if someone is interested in acting a scene, he or she has to write the script. This is pretty much the way that my own formation has been, always learning from both the experience and the challenge. In 1999, as a part of a pilot program, I created workshops for inmates with HIV in Villa Devoto's penitentiary. I believe in using creativity as a therapeutic form for people who are dealing with terminal diseases. Actually, those workshops were a very enriching experience for all participants.

MCA: After *Teatro Abierto*, have there been other similar social and cultural movements interested in promoting the dialogue among playwrights?

STM: In 1983, I was offered the artistic direction of the Teatro del Viejo Palermo, a position that I accepted with the ulterior motive of gathering creative and talented people who were scattered at the time. After running it for several months, I quit because I could not develop it any further. The original owner had very conservative ideas. However, I promptly had the opportunity to open my own space. Along with two friends, I renovated an old warehouse that became El Hangar in Palermo Viejo. Several renowned artists like Alberto Ure, Pavlovsky, Ricardo Bartis, Lorenzo Quinteros, Laura Yusem, and Lía Jelin, among others, worked and performed there. This was a very important site for alternative performance, but by 1990, the socioeconomic situation had become critical. We had to close the space due to inflation and lack of financial backing. In order to keep it running, we would have had to make concessions to our artistic selection, so after investing a considerable amount of money and effort into remodeling, we decided to return it to its owner. Through the years I have been looking for spaces in which to promote interdisciplinary approaches. There is something in me that it is constantly interested in trying to mix several artistic areas in order to find new ways of expression.

As I already mentioned, my dialogue with other dramatists is highly motivating. Susy Gutiérrez Posse, Susana Poujol, Lucía Laragione, Victor Winer, and I meet weekly to learn the difficult art of socializing information. In these meetings I became aware of the possibility of sending plays to competitions and international drama festivals. This is how I won the Premio de Dramaturgia Hermanos Machado in Seville, Spain in 1990 with *Una noche cualquiera* [Any Other Night]. In fact, meeting once a week forces us to create material to work on –because if you attend a couple of sessions empty-handed, the group begins to demand and to question your participation– so this is actually a very positive pressure, very stimulating. It is always very enriching to work in a group because you learn to respect differences, criticism, and above all, you learn to live with very different points of view and aesthetics.

In 2001, I became a member of the selection committee of *Teatroxlaidentidad*, [Theatreforidentity], an unprecedented theatre cycle sponsored by Las Abuelas de la Plaza de Mayo [The Grandmothers of the Plaza de Mayo], and that counted with the collaboration and support of several playwrights. All artistic proposals had to do with the issue of identity in its multiple interpretations. On March 24, forty-one plays were performed in fourteen theatres in the city of Buenos Aires. Everybody worked for months *ad honorem*. Along with three other playwrights, I co-wrote the show *Sorteo* [Raffle] under the direction of Ruben Pires–, and I directed María Mascheroni's *La noche sabe lo que hace cuando tiembla* [The Night Knows What It Does When It Trembles (2001)]. All through the process of creation and organization, the cycle was one of the most gratifying experiences in which I have participated in these last few years.

MCA: In your plays, how do you relate body language and writing?

STM: I do not have a recurring point of departure. Sometimes I am very inspired by reality itself; however, sometimes news that shocks me also becomes a trigger for creation. As in *Manifiesto* [Manifest (1998)], *Modus Operandi* (1999), *Lo que no se nombra* [The Unnamable (1999)], and *Nada entre los dientes* [Nothing Between the Teeth (1999)]. All these works were triggered by an initial event that stimulated my writing and my creativity. There are some plays that arise from images, texts, or a piece of music. Then I work with the actors: with them or through them. In this process, the puzzle begins to take shape. Such was the case with *Amantissima* [Beloved (1999)], *Espiral de fuego* [Spiral of Fire (1985)], and *Paraísos perdidos* [Paradises Lost (1997)]. There are other plays in which, as a playwright, I feel the need to elaborate a text, but later, in my role as a director, I don't know how I will stage the scenes. That was my experience with plays like *Unió Mystica* [Mystic Unio (1991)], *Cero* [Zero (1999)], *Estática* [Static (2000)], and *Como si nada* [As if Nothing (2000). Many times while listening to a piece of music, something bursts, something that needs to be expressed, and finally becomes apparent in writing. I don't know how the text will take shape until I hear the characters speak; only when they speak does the text begin to flow. This takes me to the realm of the body, where I listen to them, I see them, I let them be, and most important, I urge them to surprise me.

MCA: Do you think that your work follows the sociocultural discourse of contemporary Argentina, or are you inclined to work toward universal topics?

STM: Undoubtedly, there is a universal memory, but I believe that male writers and playwrights re-create a world of men, a world where women do not exist or, if they exist, their presence is poorly recognized or tinged with prejudice. This has frequently been the case with older generations of playwrights. Today's younger dramatists have a different perspective. It is important that our generation has begun to write a lot of theatre from a woman's perspective. The same happened with cinematography; originally, in this field, there were only very few women scriptwriters and directors, and that has also changed. Now there are several women authors, the ones who write from a place in which female characters are either protagonists or placed within a co-protagonistic role. Even when universal themes are addressed, there are also themes pertinent to the lives of contemporary men and women. People always share the same interests: love, death, loneliness, and existence. The main idea, however, is to address these issues from a different perspective, always original and revealing.

Obviously, culturally speaking, I have a vision trained through the feminine. When I write about male characters, I try to generate in myself a particular transmutation that cannot be explained, and that certainly belongs to the mysteries of the creative process. I have the capacity to open up to other languages and to other distant voices; such is my nature. In fact, for *Una noche cualquiera*, when the play was selected for reading at the 3rd International Women Playwrights Conference, in Adelaide, Australia, male actors were very surprised by my text because they found it amazing that a woman could write with such strength and such a clearly masculine language. I suppose that I possess the ability of being like Woody Allen's Zelig, a skill that I have perfected over the years. I observe, I listen, and I am very alert to what happens in my encounters with others.

MCA: Is it easier to project a discourse towards the feminine?

STM: For a period of time, my plays tended to project exclusively towards the feminine, as is the case with *Amantissima, Canto de Sirenas, ...Y a otra cosa mariposa* and *Unió Mystica,* but after a while, I felt the need to expand my creative vision, and I became more interested in representing a wider perspective of reality. Actually, in my most recent texts, all my characters are men. This is not something predetermined, but sometimes stories arise in which the voice, the discourse - is masculine. Then I allow it because I feel that the role of female protagonists on stage has already been done, or at least, is well on its way.

MCA: How would you like to be remembered?

STM: In fact, I recently conducted the following exercise in my workshop. Everybody had to write his or her own epitaph. I thought that mine would read: "She always tried to make her life her best work of art." Perhaps this is because I am not only interested in creating and generating artistic products, but I also want them to be incorporated into my existence and be a part of that creative energy. I intend to have a beautiful, intense, enriching life. It was Nietzsche, I believe, who said that in the world there have been great creators, but only a few who knew how to live their lives to their maximum potential. I am always trying to improve my being, my quality of life, and myself.

It is important to be aware of those enriching moments within my daily routine; otherwise, I become sick or lost in this whirlwind, in this excess of stimuli and information, which, in the end, distances me from true knowledge. It is important to know where to place my energy instead of buying into the program that the System has to offer, because what the System offers is absolutely unnecessary, mostly guided by immediacy and profit, and these have never been good parameters for achieving only but a flash of wisdom.

August 11, 2003, Buenos Aires.
Originally published in Spanish in *Latin American Literary Review*.

Strange Toy

Teatro Payró, Buenos Aires (1977)

They are playing a game.
They are playing at not playing a game.
If I show them, I see they are,
I will break the rules, and they will punish me.
I must play their game, of not seeing I see the game. (R.D. Laing, Knots)

> *On stage are two women, PERLA and ANGÉLICA. Both are between 35 and 40 years old. The entire play takes place in a living room/dining room, comfortable, but with a certain small town atmosphere.*
>
> *PERLA crosses the stage carrying glasses in her hands. She puts them in a china cabinet. She goes from one side to the other straightening and picking up things. ANGÉLICA is seated in a chair. Very slowly, she is putting on nylons. Later, she gets up, barefoot. She looks at herself in the mirror. She straightens her dress. She sits down again in front of the mirror. PERLA, having finished straightening up the room, turns toward ANGÉLICA. They look at each other for a moment. PERLA picks up a comb and begins to comb ANGÉLICA'S hair.*

ANGÉLICA: *[In a child's voice.]* Ouch! That hurts!
PERLA: You have to comb your hair more often.
ANGÉLICA: What time is it?

PERLA: Four o'clock. Why?
ANGÉLICA: I forgot! My soap opera! It's almost over! Finish! Hurry up!
PERLA: Sit still or it's going to hurt you more.
ANGÉLICA: What is this obsession you have with braiding my hair?
PERLA: It's so you look more put together.
ANGÉLICA: *[Mockingly.]* It's for your sake I'm "more put together." *[Short pause.]* I'm going to buy myself a hat.
PERLA: You're crazy! Nobody wears them anymore.
ANGÉLICA: The women in the magazines always wear hats.
PERLA: *[She finishes brushing.]* Yes, in the magazines... good, you're done.
ANGÉLICA: *[Looking at herself in the mirror.]* It's too flat. It makes my face look like a pancake.
PERLA: *[Without looking at her.]* It looks good on you.
ANGÉLICA: Did you notice? I'm going bald. *[She touches her hair.]*
PERLA: You're always saying that.
ANGÉLICA: *[Almost whimpering.]* And my shoes? Where are my shoes?
PERLA: Right in front of you. Don't you see them? Look at how disorganized you are!
ANGÉLICA: *[Excited.]* The soap opera!
PERLA: *[Menacing.]* Slow down, OK? I'm only going to say it once.
ANGÉLICA: *[Turning on the radio.]* It ends this month. The mother is very sick. *[She speaks without looking at PERLA.]*
PERLA: Who? What are you talking about?
ANGÉLICA: The mother. Doña Clotilde
PERLA: Doña Clotilde? *[Sighs.]* Who is she?
ANGÉLICA: The mother... the mother on "Blood in the Veins."
PERLA: ...

ANGÉLICA: My soap opera!

PERLA: Always the same nonsense. You never change.

ANGÉLICA: Her son is very far away. Poor thing! She doesn't know anything.

PERLA: *[Looking at herself in the mirror.]* Does this skirt make me look fat?

ANGÉLICA: *[Without looking at her.]* She wants to see him before she dies. She has something very important to tell him.

PERLA: Are you listening?

ANGÉLICA: She doesn't know where he is, nobody knows where he is.

PERLA: I asked you something, didn't I?

ANGÉLICA: *[Pause.]* She's so ill!

PERLA: Who?

ANGÉLICA: Doña Clotilde. Poor woman! At her age...! *[She squirms in her chair.]*

PERLA: *[Angry.]* Will you sit still? You'll wrinkle your dress!

[ANGÉLICA is listening to her soap opera with her ear practically pinned to the radio. PERLA takes out her knitting and begins to knit.][Pause.] Did you make the bed?

ANGÉLICA: Shut up, I can't hear! A telegram!

PERLA: I've had it with your nonsense! *[She throws a skein of yarn at her.]* Help me!

ANGÉLICA: What does she have to tell him that is so important?

PERLA: We have to cut the lawn. It's an embarrassment.

ANGÉLICA: It's from Rome. It says that he's coming.

PERLA: This morning, through the window, I saw a man looking at the house.

ANGÉLICA: Finally! Now she can die in peace!

[When turning off the radio, she tangles the yarn.]

PERLA: Be careful! Look what you're doing!
ANGÉLICA: Fine. You annoy me. It bores me to be here. *[Pause.]*
PERLA: ANGÉLICA!
ANGÉLICA: What?
PERLA: Look at me carefully. How old do I look?
ANGÉLICA: Your... age! How should I know!
PERLA: Are you sure?
ANGÉLICA: *[Suddenly interested.]* What was the man like?
PERLA: There are days that I feel so young...
ANGÉLICA: Tall?
PERLA: A little girl...
ANGÉLICA: Tall?
PERLA: *[Suspiciously.]* Yes. Why?
ANGÉLICA: With broad shoulders?
PERLA: Yes.
ANGÉLICA: About... forty years old?
PERLA: Yes... you saw him?
ANGÉLICA: *[Mysteriously.]* I don't know. He looked that way to me.
PERLA: Where?
ANGÉLICA: I don't know. *[Pause.]* It's getting dark.
PERLA: It's barely five o'clock..
ANGÉLICA: But it's already night.
PERLA: Tomorrow, bright and early, we cut the lawn.
ANGÉLICA: Ugh! Always giving orders.
PERLA: If it weren't for me, this place would be a pigsty.
ANGÉLICA: *[Slyly.]* Do you know what I dreamt last night?
PERLA: What?
ANGÉLICA: That you were dying. *[PERLA stares hard at her.]* Well, it was

only a dream.

PERLA: *[Very serious.]* What is there to eat?

ANGÉLICA: Breaded veal cutlets.

PERLA: Didn't I tell you I'm on a diet?

ANGÉLICA: I like veal cutlets.

PERLA: I like them too, but I don't want to gain weight, do you understand? *[Pause. She touches her belly.]* I want to take care of myself! *[ANGÉLICA looks down... Short pause.]* What was the dream like?

ANGÉLICA: What dream?

PERLA: My dream last night.

ANGÉLICA: *[Slyly.]* We were going to an amusement park, and we went on a roller coaster. *[Pause.]*

PERLA: And?

ANGÉLICA: Suddenly you got angry about something and you stopped and stood up in the little car...

[Longer pause.]

PERLA: What's wrong?

ANGÉLICA: I forgot...

PERLA: You have to remember. Come on! Try to remember!

ANGÉLICA: Where was I...?

PERLA: Come on! What's wrong with you? Out with it!

ANGÉLICA: *[Confused.]* Yes, you stood up in the little car... and you started to scream... and I looked at you... and suddenly... the little car went down, shush *[With her hands, she imitates a roller coaster descending.]* at full speed, and you fell out... toward the ground below *[She begins to laugh]* and while you were falling, you kept on screaming and I thought it was terribly funny, and I laughed... *[She laughs.]* I just couldn't stop laughing... *[Devilishly.]* You were so funny, falling with your legs apart.

PERLA: *[Indignant.]* What an idiot!
ANGÉLICA: *[Laughing.]* And why are you asking me?
PERLA: *[As if thinking aloud.]* Yes, I don't know why I ask you...
ANGÉLICA: You have no sense of humor. *[Pause.]* That's why they think you're older than you are.
PERLA: Who thinks I'm older?
ANGÉLICA: How should I know! People...
PERLA: What people?
ANGÉLICA: The other day in the drugstore they asked me how much older you were.
PERLA: And you didn't tell them that I was younger than you?
ANGÉLICA: What for? Who cares? *[Short pause.]*
PERLA: And who was there?
ANGÉLICA: Where?
PERLA: In the drugstore. Who was there?
ANGÉLICA: Stop it! Why do you ask so many questions? Nobody can talk to you.
PERLA: Shut up, will you?!
ANGÉLICA: And why do I have to shut up?
PERLA: Shhh... I think there's someone at the door.
[The two slowly approach the door. They stand still for a moment listening. PERLA gestures to ANGÉLICA and opens the door with a shove. Behind the door is a man with a small moustache dresses in a dark suit and black sunglasses. He is approximately 40 years old and carries a suitcase in one hand. On his other hand he wears a black glove.]
MAGGI: *[Humbly.]* Good day... Good day, ladies...
PERLA: *[Observing attentively.]* What do you want?
MAGGI: If you would be so kind, I would like to show you some novelties

that...

PERLA: *[Interrupting.]* No, thank you. We don't need anything.

ANGÉLICA: *[Anxiously.]* What's he selling? Brushes?

MAGGI: *[Disconcerted.]* Well, not exactly. *[He laughs.]* If you will just let me show you.

[He brings the suitcase forward.]

PERLA: I told you, sir, we don't need anything.

MAGGI: Well... then... *[He looks at ANGÉLICA.]*

ANGÉLICA: *[To MAGGI.]* Haven't you been here before?

MAGGI: No, ma'am... I... this is the first time I've come...

ANGÉLICA: How strange, it seemed to me that...

PERLA: *[Aggressively, to ANGÉLICA.]* What seemed to you?

ANGÉLICA: I've seen him before. His face is familiar.

MAGGI: Well, let me tell you, people say that to me all the time.

PERLA: What do they say to you?

MAGGI: That I resemble someone. *[Pause. To PERLA.]* I have a... repetitious face... *[He laughs. Longer pause. Looking at the living room.]* What a lovely room!

ANGÉLICA: You like it?

MAGGI: It has a woman's touch.

PERLA: Excuse me, but we don't have the time.

MAGGI: Just a moment...

ANGÉLICA: What do you have there?

MAGGI: *[Determined.]* Women's garments of the finest quality. If you can spare five minutes, I'll come in and show them to you without obligation.

[He makes a motion as if to enter.]

PERLA: No thank you.

ANGÉLICA: I want to see them!

MAGGI: *[To ANGÉLICA.]* OK, if you will help me, I can show them to you from here.

[He rests the suitcase on his bent right leg. ANGÉLICA helps support the suitcase and he, with his right hand only, opens the suitcase. He tries to maintain his balance.]

PERLA: *[Closing the suitcase.]* Sir, it seems we don't understand each other.

[MAGGI, teetering unsteadily, continues with the suitcase on his leg.]

MAGGI: *[To PERLA, impatiently.]* The lady asked me to show her.

ANGÉLICA: *[Opening the suitcase again.]* I want to see what he's got!

MAGGI: *[Closing the suitcase.]* Excuse me, but you're making me dizzy! *[He sets the suitcase on the ground... he laughs.]* It's an occupational hazard... *[PERLA moves to close the door.]* Please, Miss, could you bring me a glass of water, if it isn't too much trouble?*[Before PERLA can answer, ANGÉLICA goes running out of the room.]*

ANGÉLICA: Yes, of course. *[MAGGI dries his forehead with a handkerchief.]*

MAGGI: It's hot outside. *[From inside ANGÉLICA'S voice.]* Do you want ice?

MAGGI: *[Calling to ANGÉLICA.]* Good, if you will be so kind. *[To PERLA.]* Your little sister is very nice.

PERLA: *[In a foul mood.]* She's an idiot.

MAGGI: Well...even in the best families there are always some that turn out a little odd. *[He touches his hand to his head, the universal gesture indicating "crazy."]*

PERLA: What did you say? *[ANGÉLICA enters. She gives the glass of water to MAGGI. He takes his first sip.]*

MAGGI: There's nothing like water when you're thirsty. What a day! I can't stand it... out in the street... it's unbearably hot...

PERLA: Are you finished yet?

MAGGI: *[Showing the glass.]* The last sip. When I'm hot I like to drink slowly. *[He laughs.]* That's what the old woman taught me.

ANGÉLICA: What old woman?

MAGGI: My old woman. A saint! May God rest her soul. *[PERLA starts to take his glass.]* Just a minute, Miss, I'm almost finished. *[He takes the last sip.]* Thank you very much. *[PERLA stands with the glass in her hand.]* A pause is always good for one on the road. *[He laughs. He takes out his sunglasses. He looks through them, cleans them with the corner of his jacket and puts them on. He bows]* Ladies, good day! *[As he lifts the suitcase from the floor, it opens and part of his merchandise falls out.]* Damn! That lock!

ANGÉLICA: *[Looking at the clothing on the floor.]* What beautiful things!

PERLA: Oh, that's it!

MAGGI: *[Trying to fix the lock.]* She's very delicate...

PERLA: Who?

MAGGI: The suitcase. *[Pause.]* What a shame! *[ANGÉLICA is excited, looking at the merchandise. To PERLA.]* You wouldn't happen to have a screwdriver? The smaller, the better.

PERLA: Anything else? *[Leaving.]*

MAGGI: If you don't have one, I can fix it with a small knife.

ANGÉLICA: *[On her knees with a bodice in her hand.]* Mr... Mr... do you have this in my size?

MAGGI: What size are you? *[He looks at her from the corner of his eye.]* A size 6? Did I guess right?

ANGÉLICA: What skill!

MAGGI: *[Looking inside the suitcase.]* Here it is, Miss, in black. This is very fashionable.

PERLA: *[Comes back with a screwdriver.]* Here.

MAGGI: Thank you. *[He kneels down to repair the lock.]*

PERLA: *[To ANGÉLICA.]* What are you doing?

ANGÉLICA: *[Holding the bodice up to herself.]* Look at how beautiful this is!

MAGGI: *[Fixing the lock without looking at them.]* Take advantage of this opportunity, Miss. These garments are made from the finest imported nylon. Look at the label. You see? They don't need ironing. They dry in an instant and are very easily washed. Take advantage of this, I know what I'm talking about. *[To PERLA, looking at her out of the corner of his eye.]* If you'd like to look, there's no obligation.

PERLA: Do you have many sizes?

MAGGI: I simply adjust them as needed. It's no trouble.

ANGÉLICA: I'll take this one, and this one, and this one.

PERLA: But you're crazy! How are you going to pay for it all?

ANGÉLICA: The one time in my life that I buy something...

MAGGI: Don't worry about the payment... if you like it, take it, and we won't say anything more.

PERLA: ANGÉLICA, put it back!

MAGGI: Well, that's it. *[He stands up with the suitcase.]* I'm going to have to retire her... she's no good anymore. *[He begins to fold the clothing on the floor.]*

PERLA: ANGÉLICA, did you hear me?

ANGÉLICA: *[She has the garments in her hand.]* Come on, PERLA, don't be like that...

PERLA: Don't waste this man's time.

MAGGI: Time is what I have plenty of... *[To ANGÉLICA.]* Shall I leave it for you?

PERLA: Give it back! *[ANGÉLICA puts her hands behind her back.]*

MAGGI: *[To PERLA.]* Let her be, Miss...

PERLA: Mind your own business! *[To ANGÉLICA.]* Give it back! *[She makes a move to take it away from ANGÉLICA, and ANGÉLICA runs from her.]*

ANGÉLICA: I'm not going to give it back!

MAGGI: Then, I'll leave it?

PERLA: You will leave nothing!

ANGÉLICA: *[Suddenly.]* Are you sure you haven't been here before?

MAGGI: *[Disconcerted.]* I already told you, Madam, this is the first time I've been to this neighborhood...

ANGÉLICA: Are you sure?

PERLA: Why are you insisting?

ANGÉLICA: I don't know, he reminds me of someone. *[She returns the garments to MAGGI, seductively.]* If you come by another day, perhaps you'll have better luck.

PERLA: What do you mean by that?

ANGÉLICA: *[Innocently.]* Me? Nothing. Why?

PERLA: *[Very angry.]* If he comes by another day and the witch isn't here, you, you'll be sure to have yourself a real good time. Isn't that what you mean?

ANGÉLICA: I didn't say that.

PERLA: Yes, you said that. *[To MAGGI.]* Open the suitcase!

MAGGI: Madam, as far as I'm concerned...

PERLA: Didn't you hear me? Open the suitcase! *[MAGGI opens the suitcase with utmost care.]* Look, darling, there you have it! All for you! What are you waiting for? Choose! Choose! The gentleman is here to serve you... don't waste his time. *[ANGÉLICA does not move. PERLA to MAGGI.]* How odd! She's lost interest... all of a sudden... why don't you tell us what you're selling? Maybe you'll stir her enthusiasm...

MAGGI: I... if you will excuse me... *[He starts to leave.]*

PERLA: But, what kind of salesman are you!? *[Pause.]*

MAGGI: *[Disconcerted.]* Well, I have nightgowns, nylon stockings, handkerchiefs, lacy panties for that someone special, slips, shower caps...

PERLA: And what are you waiting for?

ANGÉLICA: Leave me alone.

[MAGGI continues in a monotone: "Lacy panties, handkerchiefs, nylons, slips, scarves for that someone special, nylons."]

PERLA: Stop! Stop! Can't you see that she's not interested? *[Ironically.]* You see, what happens is that my little sister is very capricious. First it's yes, later it's no.

MAGGI: *[Slamming the suitcase shut.]* Ladies, I am not here to play games... all day long you've had me opening and closing this suitcase without buying a thing. Do you want me to tell you something? I'm fed up with it! Goodbye! *[He closes the door and leaves.]*

ANGÉLICA: Congratulations! You're better at it every day.

PERLA: Thanks, dear. Your company is what inspires me. *[Short pause.]*

ANGÉLICA: Why do you always have to be so rude?

PERLA: If I don't stop you, who will?

ANGÉLICA: You're forgetting one small detail...

[They hear a knock at the door. PERLA and ANGÉLICA look at each other. ANGÉLICA moves to open the door. PERLA holds her back.]

PERLA: Stay here. I'll go.

[PERLA opens the door. MAGGI appears again with the suitcase. His expression is very serious and formal.]

PERLA: Again!

ANGÉLICA: *[Happily.]* He came back!

MAGGI: Ladies, I have come to get my satisfaction. I've been on the road for many years and never have I felt so mistreated. I am a working man and I will not allow my feelings to be toyed with. It is because I come to offer the best that I have with no intention of bothering anyone! And, at no time, will you have noticed the least sign of a lack of respect. I am a traveling salesman who expects to be treated the same way, with the same consideration. With nothing more to say, I bid you good day!

[He snatches the suitcase up quickly. It opens and everything falls out. There is an infinite variety of things. Between PERLA and ANGÉLICA falls an embalmed parrot.]

ANGÉLICA: *[Frightened.]* A creature!

PERLA: What is that? Get that out of here!

MAGGI: [Embarrassed.] Lucy!

ANGÉLICA: Who is Lucy?

MAGGI: My little parrot. *[He picks the bird up carefully from the floor. He smoothes its feathers.]* She used to travel with me.

ANGÉLICA: Is she dead?

MAGGI: Embalmed. I had her embalmed after the accident.

ANGÉLICA: Poor little thing! *[PERLA looks at her, absorbed. MAGGI, talks to the parrot in his hand. He is still caressing it.]*

MAGGI: I had her trained. I taught her to say: "Lady, Lady." They never bought so much from me! I'd grown fond of her. She ate with me. I sat down at the table and put a little plate in front of her. She was company! What more can I say?

ANGÉLICA: And what happened? *[The two sisters are most interested. MAGGI covers his face with his hands.]*

MAGGI: Don't make me remember...

ANGÉLICA: No, it's all right... if you don't want to...

MAGGI: *[Becoming enthusiastic.]* One afternoon I can't find her. I look and look and, nothing. I find this very strange because she was always at my side. The first thing I thought was that some son of a bitch had taken her... *[He makes gestures with his hand like a robber.]* I was half crazed. I shouted "Lucy, Lucy," I named her after my younger sister... well, since she didn't appear... I climbed into my car and started it up... what a mistake!

ANGÉLICA: *[Very excited.]* You ran over her!

MAGGI: Poor thing! She had been sleeping under the car... because of the heat... in summer she would sweat a lot... Poor little Lucy! She stayed alive for quite a while, and wouldn't stop calling "Lady, lady." I had to kill her.

ANGÉLICA: *[Impressed.]* You!

MAGGI: Yes. *[To the parrot.]* Forgive me, little Lucy.

ANGÉLICA: *[Curious.]* And how did you do it?

MAGGI: Do what?

ANGÉLICA: How did you...

MAGGI: Ah... a twist of the neck... like with chickens... it's the quickest. *[Pause]* Because of this I don't want any more pets. *[PERLA shudders.]*

ANGÉLICA: And, yes, one gets attached and it's hard to...

MAGGI: That's what I tell myself... When things were going well I bought her colored ribbons and put them around her neck... I still have the last one... I took it off her before I... *[He makes the gesture of a blow with his hands.]* ... so it wouldn't get dirty. *[Pause.]* If only I had taped her. Business would have been great! *[Pause.]* What a shame!

[There is a pause. The two sisters are almost hypnotized by his tale and by the presence of the parrot. MAGGI stares into space while murmuring something. PERLA draws nearer to him.]

PERLA: Is something wrong?

MAGGI: *[Pointing to the suitcase.]* Look at this mess! And what do I do now?

ANGÉLICA: *[Pointing at the parrot.]* May I borrow her?

MAGGI: What?
ANGÉLICA: May I borrow her?
MAGGI: *[Hesitating.]* Yes... but please, be careful. *[He gives her the parrot.]*
PERLA: The lock again?
MAGGI: What a shame! Suitcases today don't even last two months. *[With a fuss.]* National Lock!
PERLA: Don't you have a warranty?
MAGGI: Yes, but it's expired.
PERLA: If you want to come in and fix it here...
MAGGI: No, no thank you. I don't want to inconvenience you.
PERLA: You're not going to be able to fix it out in the street. Come in.
MAGGI: Well, OK, I'm very grateful.
[Quickly he stuffs all the fallen things back into the suitcase. Since it won't close, he carries it under his arm. At the threshold of the house, PERLA points out a large pair of slippers.]
PERLA: If you please...
MAGGI: What?
PERLA: The slippers.
MAGGI: Do I have to take off my shoes?
PERLA: No, no, put those on over them. Do you want something to drink?
MAGGI: Thank you. You're very kind.
[MAGGI puts on the slippers. He walks with some difficulty carrying the suitcase under his arm, trying to keep the slippers on. He stops in the entryway. PERLA goes to look for a glass in the living room. ANGÉLICA looks at the parrot from all angles.]
ANGÉLICA: *[About the parrot.]* What beautiful eyes!

MAGGI: *[Batting his eyelashes.]* You like them? *[He realizes that her comments are not for him, but rather for the parrot.]* Yes, she had beautiful eyes! When we ate I always told her that. *[PERLA gives him the glass. MAGGI'S right hand is occupied with the suitcase. He moves the suitcase to his left hand and puts it under his arm. He takes the glass.]*

MAGGI: *[Looking at the glass suspiciously.]* What is it?

PERLA: Port wine. We always have a little after dinner.

ANGÉLICA: *[About PERLA.]* She says it helps digestion. As for me... *[She makes a sour face.]*

MAGGI: *[To Angelica.]* Oh really? *[To PERLA.]* Thank you, you're very kind. *[MAGGI remains standing in the hallway with the pair of huge slippers on his feet. The glass in one hand, the suitcase under his arm. He takes a sip.]*

MAGGI: Beautiful place, eh? One lives well here. Is this yours?

PERLA: It's our parent's. But they've passed away.

MAGGI: Both of them?

ANGÉLICA: No, first one and later the other. *[She sets the parrot on a piece of furniture.]*

PERLA: They could never live apart.

ANGÉLICA: The house is too big. You can never find anything.

MAGGI: This is the good life. That's coming from one who lives on the street. *[He takes a sip.]* People don't know how to live. You two would be horrified to see the things that I see. Houses that look like palaces from outside and inside are rat's nests.

ANGÉLICA: *[Frightened.]* Rats?

PERLA: Are you serious?

MAGGI: I swear to you. Rat's nests. Very elegant ladies with small children that they feed stone soup to every day!

PERLA: I would have reported them.

MAGGI: With all the work the police have now, what is there to report? But Miss, please!... Ok, I'm going to tell you something else. Once I met a family, to look at them, you'd think they were millionaires. And do you know what they did at night?
ANGÉLICA: *[Excited.]* They took drugs!
MAGGI: No, Miss! They went looking through garbage cans.
PERLA: I can't believe it!
MAGGI: Yes, believe me, Miss. I swear to God. *[He crosses himself.]* They didn't spend a cent on food. Why should I lie to you?
[The suitcase slides down and he moves it back up under his arm.]
ANGÉLICA: How disgusting!
MAGGI: The things that one sees in the street. This job is like a taxi driver's. When you're working out there you get to know the life of every poor devil. What can I say? *[He takes another drink.]* I say this because I have seen so much. If not, I wouldn't say anything.
PERLA: Men have that advantage.
MAGGI: What advantage?
PERLA: Moving around so freely without anyone thinking badly of them.
MAGGI: Look, Miss, you women always say the same thing, but I, what can I say, when at night I have to check into any old run-down hotel and I have to eat alone, reheated food, and I go through three pairs of shoes a month, walking for days in the rain, what more can I say? *[He becomes aggressive.]* And you here, listening to music, knitting, preparing fancy little dishes in your little palace... look, really... what can I say? I with this liberty that men have, do you know what I do? *[He makes a rude gesture.]*
PERLA: Sir!
MAGGI: *[He gives her his hand.]* MAGGI, please to meet you. *[PERLA, confused, gives him her hand.]* Celestino MAGGI, with two g's.

ANGÉLICA: An Italian!

MAGGI: Sicilian. *[He turns to take the suitcase. Short pause.]* What happens is that you made me think of my old woman... God rest her soul. You could be related. She raised nine, and on top of that, helped out the old man. A saint!

ANGÉLICA: Did you love her very much?

MAGGI: How could I not love her? A saint! Like you two! *[He brings his hands together.]* For that reason, what can I say, a woman's life has its difficulties, but it also has its advantages.

[He gives the empty glass to PERLA.]

PERLA: A little more?

MAGGI: No, no thank you. I don't drink during working hours.

ANGÉLICA: Why don't you sit down?

MAGGI: Thank you. I'll use this opportunity to fix the lock... if it's OK with you. *[He lowers the suitcase. He looks all around because there is no chair for him.]*

[After a while.]

PERLA: ANGÉLICA, the man is waiting to sit down.

[She takes out a very small stool from underneath a piece of furniture. MAGGI goes to sit down. When he starts to walk, he looks like he is skiing. When he sits, he is visibly lower than the two sisters. Long pause. MAGGI, while seated, tries to relax; he cracks his shoulders, his neck. PERLA goes toward the sideboard. She takes out a glass. ANGÉLICA, seated, takes off her shoes and wiggles her toes. PERLA stops drinking. She leaves the glass in the sideboard. She clears her throat and returns to where the others are. ANGÉLICA puts her shoes back on while MAGGI remains quiet on his stool.]

MAGGI: Well, let's get to work!

[He begins to work on the suitcase. He takes out an incredible number of tools,

even a car jack that's good for putting the suitcase on one end. The rest of the dialogue is spoken with MAGGI continually working on the suitcase.]

PERLA: Mr. MAGGI, is it easy to sell things to women?

MAGGI: Well... one gets by... one does what one can.

PERLA: Do they always treat you well?

MAGGI: Like a king!

PERLA: Well, you're very lucky.

MAGGI: It's my looks. My face inspires confidence.

ANGÉLICA: And furthermore, you have a fine speaking voice.

MAGGI: *[Proudly.]* They always tell me that.

ANGÉLICA: Your wife... doesn't it bother her that you travel so much?

PERLA: Don't be impertinent!

MAGGI: *[To PERLA.]* Please, Miss. *[To ANGÉLICA.]* Well... I'm still unconquered.

ANGÉLICA: Unconquered?

PERLA: Yes, he still isn't...

ANGÉLICA: Ah...

MAGGI: It's not that I don't want to be, what can I say...sometimes I feel so lonely. But all this, married one day, unmarried the next... I don't know... it's all well and good for the artists, and those in their league... but one who walks off the beaten path... can't afford those sorts of luxuries, can he?

ANGÉLICA: *[Enthusiastically.]* Did you hear that Elizabeth Taylor got married again? *[PERLA makes a gesture of annoyance.]*

MAGGI: That's the way the English are...

ANGÉLICA: I have the soul of an artist. It's in my blood.

MAGGI: Do you have relatives in the theatre?

PERLA: Where?

MAGGI: In the community...

ANGÉLICA: What community?

MAGGI: *[Impatiently.]* In the community... Madam, in the artistic community.

ANGÉLICA: Ah, yes, mother played the harp.

PERLA: Well, let me tell you that we never got to listen to her because she sold the harp before she and father were married. But she always told us how they applauded her. In her day, she was a child prodigy.

MAGGI: That's great! And what do you do? Do you play anything?

ANGÉLICA: I study the dramatic arts... by mail.

PERLA: *[Laughing.]* She's waiting for Spielberg to call her to make a movie.

ANGÉLICA: You're just jealous!

PERLA: And you're off your rocker.

MAGGI: And I'm an Aquarius!

PERLA: *[Pause.]* And what does that have to do with anything?

MAGGI: *[Confused.]* Weren't you talking about astrology?

PERLA: *[Indignant.]* No, Mr. MAGGI, we were not talking about astrology.

MAGGI: No, I thought I heard...

[ANGÉLICA says the text at high speed, in a monotone, right to MAGGI'S face.]

ANGÉLICA: Aquarius men are very dangerous... they always get what they want... they are strong... impulsive... they stop at nothing...

[MAGGI is still confused. He looks at PERLA. Uncomfortable pause. MAGGI begins to search nervously for something in his pockets.]

PERLA: *[To MAGGI.]* So, you're an Aquarius? How great, eh, an Aquarius!

MAGGI: Yes, an Aquarius. What do you do? *[Tense pause.]* Ladies, if...

ANGÉLICA: *[Interrupting him.]* I'm going to work on the radio.

MAGGI: *[Relieved.]* That wouldn't be easy... I mean... to get in.

ANGÉLICA: Everybody says that I have a beautiful voice.

MAGGI: I was about to tell you that, Miss.

PERLA: *[To MAGGI.]* What were you about to tell her?

MAGGI: What?

ANGÉLICA: *[To PERLA, challengingly.]* He was telling me that I have a beautiful voice.

MAGGI: Do you sing?

ANGÉLICA: I recite.

MAGGI: That's great! *[Pause.]* When I was a boy, I loved the circus. I wanted to be a trapeze artist.

[ANGÉLICA is moving her foot.]

PERLA: Could you stop moving your foot? I can't hear.

ANGÉLICA: But I'm not making any noise.

PERLA: You're distracting me and I can't understand what he's saying. *[She points to MAGGI.]*

ANGÉLICA: As if you ever understand anything.

PERLA: What did you say?

ANGÉLICA: *[As if she didn't hear.]* So, you wanted to be a trapeze artist? How dangerous!

MAGGI: Yes, but I have a fear of heights... vertigo, they call it. That's why I do this. *[He strokes the suitcase. Long and uncomfortable pause.]*

ANGÉLICA: It's been a long time since we've had a guest.

PERLA: You are an exception, Mr. MAGGI.

ANGÉLICA: Why don't you rest a while?

MAGGI: No, I can't let grass grow under my feet. *[He smiles.]*

PERLA: Mr. MAGGI is surely a very busy man.

MAGGI: And...business is business. If one doesn't stay busy... *[Pause.]*

And do either of you work?

[ANGÉLICA gets up. She goes toward the radio. She turns it on very slowly. She sits down. She takes off her shoes again. While she listens, she sucks on her thumb. She twirls her hair with her other hand.]

PERLA: Ask me. Because as far as she's concerned...

MAGGI: *[Laughing at ANGÉLICA.]* So, she doesn't take to the yoke very well?

PERLA: The what?

MAGGI: The yoke. To bend her neck...to be burdened.

PERLA: *[Looking at him, disconcerted.]* Look, what she doesn't like is work. She was born useless and she will die useless. On the other hand, I... I could have almost been an accountant. As soon as I graduated, I went to work for an accounting firm. And not by recommendation, OK? I competed for it! I worked there seven years. Then we had the misfortune you already know about. And, as you can imagine, I couldn't let the house fall into the hands of some common idiot. I had to leave my job. You can't know how hard that was. They were my family. On my last day, they gave me a going-away party, with food and everything. We toasted. The manger of my section gave me this medal. *[She shows him a medal that she has hanging around her neck. She motions him closer.]* Read. Read the inscription.

MAGGI: I don't see anything.

PERLA: Wait, I have my magnifying glass. *[She goes to look for it. When she finds it, she gives it to him.]*

MAGGI: *[Reading.]* "To Miss PERLA, for her love and dedication during seven years of arduous labor." How beautiful, like a diploma!

PERLA: *[Emotional.]* I will never forget that day. *[She sighs.]* Now I work here. I dress mannequins that I sell to wholesalers. And that's how, by the way, I manage this. If it weren't for me, this house would just fall apart. Sometimes I ask myself: "Why do I make these sacrifices? What for?"

MAGGI: And... *[Pointing to ANGÉLICA, who is still sucking her thumb and twirling her hair]* she doesn't help you?

PERLA: Look at her! All day she's like that. Glued to the radio. Do you know what she does? She imitates the voices of the actresses. She says that she has to be ready in case they call her.

[ANGÉLICA turns off the radio and goes toward them.]

MAGGI: Yes, seven years is a lifetime.

ANGÉLICA: *[To MAGGI.]* Has she shown you her medal yet?

MAGGI: Yes, it's very beautiful.

ANGÉLICA: Her boss gave it to her before he fired her. As a compensation.

PERLA: Will you shut up!

ANGÉLICA: She had fallen in love with him and she couldn't leave him alone.

[PERLA gestures to MAGGI that ANGÉLICA is crazy.] He even had fights with his wife. *[She is very amused.]*

PERLA: *[To MAGGI.]* She's like that because she listens to soap operas all day long.

ANGÉLICA: *[Laughing.]* The whole world knew!

MAGGI: *[Uncomfortable.]* And you, Miss... *[To ANGÉLICA]* don't you have a boyfriend?

ANGÉLICA: I used to... but we fought... he was very jealous.

PERLA: A random lunatic. He never wanted to come to the house.

MAGGI: *[Laughing.]* He probably didn't want to put on those slippers.

[The two sisters look at him seriously. MAGGI tries to fix the situation.]

And, of course, if your boyfriend is jealous... after you're married, mama mía!

ANGÉLICA: He didn't want me to study acting.

MAGGI: Because of all the fame?

ANGÉLICA: What fame? Nobody knows who I am.

MAGGI: No, I mean because of the bad reputation.

ANGÉLICA: What are you saying?

MAGGI: No, what I mean is, they say, actresses have a bad reputation.

ANGÉLICA: Ah, you think just the way he did.

MAGGI: No, not me. As far as I'm concerned, everyone should do what they want. *[Short pause.]* Look, I have a sister who sings tango songs. So, how can I think that?

PERLA: What's your sister's name?

MAGGI: No, no, she's not well known. She just started. *[Pause.]* But she'll succeed! You just remember what I said.

ANGÉLICA: I'm hoping for that.

MAGGI: For whom?

ANGÉLICA: The stars say that my moment hasn't come yet. But it's close, very close.

PERLA: *[Bearing down on her.]* Tell the stars to hurry up. If they don't, you'll be working as a grandmother. *[To MAGGI.]* She doesn't lift a finger without consulting the stars.

MAGGI: And that's the way it should be. What can I say: everyone gets by as best they can. *[Out of the suitcase falls some women's clothing.]*

ANGÉLICA: *[Impulsively.]* Can I see?

MAGGI: *[Teasingly.]* But I don't want the same thing to happen again.

PERLA: Will you control yourself!

MAGGI: *[To PERLA.]* Leave her be, let her enjoy. Life is short, let her enjoy it.

[ANGÉLICA takes a shower cap from the suitcase.]

MAGGI: If you don't like that one, I have three different models. Try it on, no obligation.

[ANGÉLICA tries it on. MAGGI turns the suitcase around and takes out another

one. ANGÉLICA *tries that one on, too. This goes on a few more times. MAGGI looks at her from the corner of his eye while fussing with his suitcase.]*
MAGGI: *[Without looking at them.]* If I may offer my personal opinion, that one really suits you. I usually don't tell my customers this, but that really looks good on you. Not on everyone, eh.
[ANGÉLICA parades around the room, modeling her shower cap. There is in her a very playful provocative attitude.]
What can I say? I'm in love with the clothes I sell. Miss PERLA, you are so very nice... look at this nightgown. Do you like it? *[He gives it to her.]* Look at yourself in the mirror.
[PERLA very modestly takes the nightgown from him and covers herself with it, as if she were naked. She doesn't go to the mirror. She is transfixed.]
What do you say, eh? The truth is I wasn't born to be a salesman. As far as I am concerned, I would give this all way. I am a lover of good taste. *[To ANGÉLICA, looking at her from the corner of his eye.]* If I were Spielberg! Do you know something? You two really compliment the décor of this house. You look just like two little dolls. Two precious little dolls!
[When MAGGI says that, the two sisters look at each other. PERLA reacts, dropping the nightgown on the suitcase and going to the cabinet. ANGÉLICA takes off the shower cap. She sits down and takes off her shoes. MAGGI sets down the suitcase. He stays quiet for an instant on his stool. Secretly, he takes a piece of paper out of his pocket. He reads it and puts it back in his pocket.]
MAGGI: Excuse me, is there a bathroom here?
PERLA: *[Pointing to a door that adjoins the living room.]* Through that door, in the back.
ANGÉLICA: Don't be crazy. Let him go to the other bathroom.
PERLA: Why do we have a guest bathroom?
ANGÉLICA: I don't know. Because nobody ever comes here.

PERLA: And Mr. MAGGI, what is he? *[ANGÉLICA does not answer.]* Let's see... tell me, what is he?

ANGÉLICA: *[With a fuss.]* A guest.

PERLA: *[Triumphant.]* And which bathroom does he have to use?

ANGÉLICA: *[With even more of a fuss.]* The one for visitors!

PERLA: *[Triumphantly, pointing again to the door.]* Mr. MAGGI!

[MAGGI has been listening to the dialogue very attentively. He stands up. He straightens the crease in his pants. He tries to slide himself along the floor with the slippers, but cannot. He feels ridiculous and walks, lifting his feet as if he wore skis. He has a visible tag hanging from the seat of his pants. He crosses the entire stage and disappears through the door.]

[PERLA stands up and goes to the cabinet. She pours herself a drink. Meanwhile, ANGÉLICA takes out a bottle of perfume. She dabs some behind her ears, along her neck, and between her breasts.]

ANGÉLICA: Did you put toilet paper in the guest bathroom?

PERLA: I told you that was your job.

ANGÉLICA: You know I never go in that bathroom.

PERLA: *[Ironically.]* Really?

ANGÉLICA: Only when I want to read in peace. *[She puts a breath mint in her mouth.]*

PERLA: *[Laughing.]* Read what? Love letters?

ANGÉLICA: *[Irritated.]* Shut up, you lush!

[PERLA hurls the glass at her. The glass hits against the wall nearest the bathroom.]

MAGGI: *[Opening the bathroom door.]* What's going on?

PERLA: *[Peacefully.]* Nothing. Something fell.

MAGGI: Ah! *[He turns and closes the bathroom door.]*

PERLA: Go get a broom!

ANGÉLICA: I didn't break it!

PERLA: And what does that have to do with it? Go!

[ANGÉLICA, in a bad mood, goes to look for a broom. She brings one back and begins to sweep up the glass. PERLA is content and hums to herself. MAGGI comes out of the bathroom. He no longer has the tag on his pants. He comes out adjusting his glove. PERLA and ANGÉLICA look at him. MAGGI crosses the entire stage and sits down again on the stool at the side of the hall. He continues working on repairing his suitcase.]

MAGGI: *[Timidly, pointing at the bathroom.]* There isn't any light or water.

PERLA: That bathroom is a disaster. There's never anything there.

ANGÉLICA: *[Still sweeping.]* Why do you wear that glove, Mr. MAGGI?

MAGGI: *[To ANGÉLICA, as if he hadn't heard her.]* You wouldn't happen to have a hairpin?

ANGÉLICA: A hairpin?

MAGGI: Yes, if you would be so kind. *[To PERLA.]* It's a good thing I have two.

PERLA: Two what?

MAGGI: Two suitcases. I use this one in the afternoon. And when I go out at night, I have another one.

[MAGGI opens and closes the suitcase, making a lot of irritating noise.]

PERLA: Mr. MAGGI, please. You're hurting my ears!

MAGGI: I'm sorry. It's a habit.

ANGÉLICA: *[She gives him the hairpin.]* Do you always wear that glove?

MAGGI: Yes, Miss. *[To PERLA.]* The clientele in the evening expect another thing entirely. Completely different merchandise. It's a different world. *[To ANGÉLICA.]* And the hairpin?

ANGÉLICA: You have it in your hand.

PERLA: And what do you sell?

MAGGI: *[Cleaning out his ear with the hairpin.]* If you knew the things I have to sell! And...my evening customers aren't at all like you. They're different people. Usually it's men that I sell to. At bars, nightclubs. Night people. *[Looking at the hairpin.]* They'll buy anything! But, what's the point of telling you? And the prices! They pay whatever I ask!

ANGÉLICA: *[Who has never stopped looking at the glove.]* Do you always wear only one?

MAGGI: *[Annoyed.]* Yes, Miss. I always wear only one. *[He grabs hold of the suitcase and beats it.]* It looks like it won't last much longer.

ANGÉLICA: And why do you wear only one?

PERLA: How tedious you are!

ANGÉLICA: What's wrong with asking him?

MAGGI: Nothing, Miss. *[Patiently.]* The thing is, if you ask me about the glove, I have to talk about the accident, and I would prefer not to.

PERLA: The accident?

MAGGI: *[Resigned.]* You see, it's always the same. You end up talking about what you'd rather not discuss.

PERLA: You're right. My father, who had a glass eye, always used to say: *[ANGÉLICA repeats it with her, as if it were a lesson well-learned.]* "The shame is not in the defect, but rather in people's curiosity about it."

ANGÉLICA: *[To MAGGI.]* Did she tell you that her boss looked like father?

[PERLA stares at her coldly. ANGÉLICA pretends not to understand.]

MAGGI: *[Trying to change the situation.]* Your father was right! Tell me, what happened to the old man?

PERLA: A horse...

MAGGI: *[Interrupting her.]* What, he was trampled?

PERLA: No, because he was looking at a horse, he ran into a post.

MAGGI: Oh, the poor fellow! Which eye?

PERLA: The left.

MAGGI: That's not so bad. At least he still had the right.

[MAGGI takes the suitcase. He stops, and without moving from where he stands, shakes it to see if it will fall open. He does this a few more times. Meanwhile, ANGÉLICA sprays the room with a deodorizer.]

PERLA: Is that it?

MAGGI: I want to make sure. Once it opened up out on the street. They grabbed everything, right down to my thimbles! And I, on top of it all, with this hand...

ANGÉLICA: What? You can't move it?

MAGGI: I can't defend myself! Otherwise...

PERLA: Otherwise what?

MAGGI: I'd kill them! I'd beat them so hard their own mothers wouldn't recognize them!

[Silence. The three stare at each other.]

MAGGI: *[Bothered.]* Why are you staring at me?

PERLA: No, you're staring at us.

MAGGI: Ah! *[Pause.]* OK, if you want, I'll tell you.

ANGÉLICA: Tell us what, Mr. MAGGI?

MAGGI: About the accident. But I must warn you, it's not a pretty story. *[He begins opening and closing the suitcase.]*

ANGÉLICA: You don't have to tell me the story. I just wanted to know why you wear the glove.

PERLA: You always do that! Questions, questions, and more questions... and then you look as if butter couldn't melt in your mouth!

[MAGGI, who had become disinterested in the conversation, continues testing his suitcase.] What are you doing? You're going to break it again!

MAGGI: I'm a little obsessive about these things. *[He sets it down on the *floor.]* Well, there it is. *[He stops. He adjusts his pants.]* Now, off to work!

PERLA: What? Are you leaving?

MAGGI: Yes. Why? Did you need something?

PERLA: I thought you were going to tell us...

[ANGÉLICA bursts out laughing. PERLA pays her no attention.]

MAGGI: Tell you what?

PERLA: What happened to you.

MAGGI: Ah, what happened to me... *[His attitude changes brusquely.]* Excuse me, Miss, but I've already lost a lot of time. We'll leave that for another day.

PERLA: It'll only take five more minutes. What will that cost you?

ANGÉLICA: My, how tedious *you* are, eh?

MAGGI: What time is it?

PERLA: It's early.

ANGÉLICA: It's almost dark.

MAGGI: Do you have a telephone?

ANGÉLICA: Yes, but it hasn't worked in six months.

MAGGI: It might be because of the rain... the cables swell up. Does it rain much here?

ANGÉLICA: Every once in a while. *[Bored.]*

MAGGI: You're lucky. Here you can breathe. Well, I won't keep you waiting any longer. *[He extends his hand to them.]*

PERLA: *[Determined.]* Mr. MAGGI, what happened?

[There is a long pause as the three stare at each other. PERLA'S attitude is "he's not leaving here without telling the story." ANGÉLICA remains an observer. MAGGI very slowly lowers the suitcase and sits down on the stool again. He adjusts the crease in his pants. PERLA brings a chair and sits down. She looks at

ANGÉLICA, who is still standing and watching. ANGÉLICA sits down on the floor. She rests her head on PERLA'S lap and begins sucking her thumb and twirling her hair again.]

MAGGI: It was a long time ago. I was ten years old. My old man had a little market. A lovely little place. It was the pride of the neighborhood! Clean! Orderly! I always helped him stock the fruit. It was an art because you had to stock the fruit in such a way that the rotten stuff always stayed covered up.

[The two sisters can't take their eyes off him.]

One afternoon, all of us little kids got together... I can almost see it now...! We started to play "storekeeper"... some of the kids got in line, and another waited on them. That job went to me. It was all going well. We were having a terrific time. Until it came to a turn for... for...

PERLA: *[Anxiously.]* For...

ANGÉLICA: *[Content.]* He forgot!

PERLA: Shut up! You're making him nervous!

[MAGGI looks nervously for something in his pocket.]

MAGGI: For... Carlitos... *[Relieved.]* Yes, Carlitos! *[As if speaking to Carlitos.]* And what do you want? *[He stares directly at the sisters and they look at each other.]* Cold cuts! *[He looks sharply at them again.]* And do you know why? Because that little son of a... excuse me, that little Carlitos decided I didn't know how to use the cutting machine and he wanted to see me cut him a slice. You had to watch out because the cutting machine was electric!

ANGÉLICA: *[Taking her thumb out of her mouth.]* Electric!

PERLA: That's it!

MAGGI: Made in Germany! I, as if it were nothing, grabbed some baked ham. I put it in the machine. I don't know how... it just started up by itself.

PERLA: And them...? Go on! Go on!

MAGGI: And...I was scared because the baked ham wasn't placed in there right and the machine was just tearing it apart. And, remember, OK, a baked ham is no plaything!

ANGÉLICA: No, of course not!

PERLA: And...

MAGGI: And then... I tried to take it out, but I didn't know how to stop the machine... and I guessed wrong...

PERLA: *[On the edge of her chair.]* And...

ANGÉLICA: *[Stopping herself.]* No more, please!

MAGGI: In an instant, four of my fingers flew away!

ANGÉLICA: Four!

PERLA: You were lucky you didn't lose them all.

MAGGI: *[Enthusiastic.]* How that damned thing cut! What a blade it had! My old man said it could split a hair in two. German! Over there they know how to make things, but not here.

PERLA: And... what happened after...

ANGÉLICA: Stop it! Please!

MAGGI: *[Lost in thought.]* There was blood all over the store. The kids, of course, ran out of there in a hurry. They left me alone. I didn't know whether I was crying for my hand, or for my old man's ham, all torn up. Mama mía, what a scene! I jumped up and down like a madman, and my four fingers stuck together, stuck together, one next to the other, on top of the ham. My old man, he almost fainted. *[Pause.]* Later, they fixed me up, and I came out pretty well. *[Pause. He turns and faces them]* If you like, I'll show them to you?

ANGÉLICA: If you don't mind.

PERLA: No, no thank you. I'm too easily affected. *[Pause.]* Why don't you go on with your story?

ANGÉLICA: But first, let us see it. It shouldn't be that bad.

MAGGI: So, what's your decision?

ANGÉLICA: I want to see it!
PERLA: Tell me, what did you feel?
ANGÉLICA: *[Like a capricious little girl.]* Come on! Show us!
PERLA: Tell us! Tell us!
MAGGI: *[Inhaling, throws his shoulders back.]* Please, ladies. Make up your minds!
ANGÉLICA: We already know... he likes us to beg him.
PERLA: He can count on us.
ANGÉLICA: Doesn't he count on us?
PERLA: Of course. We're two strangers. Isn't that true?
ANGÉLICA: However, we open our doors to him.
PERLA: And we listen attentively to him.
ANGÉLICA: We even confide our secrets to him.
PERLA: Because we took him to be a gentleman.
ANGÉLICA: So then...?
PERLA: What's wrong with him?
MAGGI: *[Confused.]* With me? Nothing. *[With a certain anger.]* Look, I'll show you! And then I'll continue telling the story. So, we finish it, OK?
ANGÉLICA: That sounds fine to me.
PERLA: Let me say it again, Mr. MAGGI... I do not want to see it!
MAGGI: But Miss, I don't understand. We're all adults.
PERLA: *[Standing up.]* I forbid you to show it to me!
ANGÉLICA: Don't pay any attention to her. She's always overreacting.
MAGGI: No, but she has her rights. If she doesn't want to see it, she doesn't have to.
ANGÉLICA: And...what are you waiting for?
MAGGI: Me?
ANGÉLICA: Aren't you going to show it to me?

PERLA: Fine. If you want me to leave, I'm going.

MAGGI: Don't take it that way, Miss PERLA. Please, ladies, calm down. *[Short pause.]* Look, I just got an idea. Let's see what you think of it. [Pause.] I'll show it under the table... and the person who wants to look, looks. *[He looks at both of them.]* What do you say? *[The two sisters look at him without saying a word. MAGGI, with his hand under the table.]* Are you ready? One... two...

PERLA: *[Interrupting him.]* Wait, one little question... if... if... I wanted... just out of curiosity... it's not that... I'm interested... but... well... you know how women are... if... I... would like... would I be able to touch it...?

MAGGI: Naturally! That's what it's for! *[He looks first at one, then the other, with a big smile on his face.]* One... two... thr... *[MAGGI begins to take off his glove under the table. ANGÉLICA wants to help him. MAGGI asks her to stay still because he's ticklish. Meanwhile, PERLA slowly brings her hand to the table. The scene reaches a crescendo between the smiles of MAGGI and the excitement of the sisters until MAGGI tells them to look. ANGÉLICA furtively looks under the table. She falls to the floor, twitching and convulsing--then she's still. MAGGI brings his hand up, with the glove back on]* Did you see? I warned you. That's why I didn't want to tell you.

PERLA: Don't worry about it. This happens to her all the time. Will you help me?

MAGGI: Sure, why not. Where do we put her?

PERLA: Over this way.

[They pick ANGÉLICA up by her arms and legs and enter the living room. They seat her in a chair. PERLA goes to the cabinet and makes herself a drink. While she does this, she murmurs quietly to herself. MAGGI goes to look for his suitcase in the hall. ANGÉLICA, opening her eyes and speaking mechanically, as if she had a nervous tick.]

ANGÉLICA: Where are my shoes?

PERLA: *[Ironically.]* Welcome!

[ANGÉLICA, paying no attention to her sister, gets up and goes toward her assortment of perfumes. She begins spraying herself in a very frantic, almost hysterical way. MAGGI remains standing in the middle of the living room with his suitcase in his hand. He observes the scene.]

MAGGI: It's so precious! So precious!

PERLA: Please, Mr. MAGGI. Make yourself comfortable.

MAGGI: I appreciate that, Miss. But... *[He looks at his watch. PERLA is insistent and MAGGI doesn't know what to do.]* Well, that's it. The whole day is lost!

[PERLA points to the stool that is still in the hall. MAGGI goes and brings it back. He sits down. Pause. Slowly, MAGGI takes a bag of tobacco out of one pocket and a pipe from the other. With utmost care, he prepares his pipe.]

PERLA: Mr. MAGGI... do late Sunday afternoons also make you sad?

[ANGÉLICA, meanwhile, has set up a chessboard on the table and is arranging the pieces.]

ANGÉLICA: *[To PERLA.]* Why do you say, "also?"

PERLA: *[To ANGÉLICA.]* I meant to ask if he also gets sad in the late afternoon on Sundays.

[MAGGI, meanwhile, prepares the pipe. He observes the dialogue uncomfortably. PERLA sits down in front of ANGÉLICA and begins to play chess with her while conversing.]

ANGÉLICA: *[To PERLA.]* But first, you have to ask him, before you can say "also."

PERLA: *[Moving a piece.]* Who?

ANGÉLICA: *[Staring intently at the board.]* Mr. MAGGI.

PERLA: *[Also concentrating on the game.]* And just whom *am* I talking to?

ANGÉLICA: *[Moving a piece.]* What I'm saying is, that when someone says "also," he is referring to someone who has already said something. And until now, Mr... .Mr...

MAGGI: MAGGI!

ANGÉLICA: Ah, yes. Mr. MAGGI hasn't opened his mouth. *[Looking accusingly at MAGGI.]* Isn't that so? *[Immediately she returns her gaze to the chessboard.]*

MAGGI: What?

PERLA: *[Looking at MAGGI.]* Ah, isn't that so? *[She moves a piece.]*

MAGGI: *[Confused.]* Well, it could be.

[MAGGI has already finished packing his pipe, but each time he is about to put it in his mouth, the two sisters lay into him with their questions, baiting and confusing him.]

ANGÉLICA: *[Moving a piece.]* Did you speak of your sadness on Sundays before my sister brought up the topic?

MAGGI: *[Taking the pipe out of his mouth.]* No, I don't think so.

ANGÉLICA: Then this is the first time we've talked about this matter?

MAGGI: Yes... *[He tries to light the pipe.]*

ANGÉLICA: *[Energetically.]* Then, don't you think that the word "also" is a bit out of place in a topic that's *never* been brought up before?

MAGGI: *[He lowers his pipe without lighting it.]* Look, Miss, really, I don't pay attention to so many details. *[He raises the pipe again.]*

PERLA: *[Moving a piece.]* What details?

[MAGGI lowers his pipe again.]

ANGÉLICA: Are you referring to the sadness as a detail?

PERLA: Or to Sundays?

MAGGI: *[Totally disoriented.]* What? *[He has a lit match in his hand.]*

ANGÉLICA: *[Moving a piece.]* To the sadness?

PERLA: Or to Sundays?

ANGÉLICA: *[Looking at him from the corner of her eye.]* What happens to you "also?"

PERLA: *[Moving a piece.]* You can see it on his face.

[MAGGI, with the lit match in his hand, observes the dialogue without doing anything. Suddenly there is an expression of pain on his face. He has burned himself.]

ANGÉLICA: *[Very consumed with the chess game.]* He has melancholy eyes.

PERLA: A sad look. Resigned.

[MAGGI, meanwhile runs his fingers through his hair with a grimace of pain.]

ANGÉLICA: *[Moving a piece.]* Let him speak!

PERLA: But he doesn't talk! *[Moving a piece.]*

MAGGI: *[With great effort, and in a higher voice than normal.]* After the parties' broadcast is over! *[He lights his pipe.]*

PERLA: *[Jumping to her feet, frightened.]* We are not interested in party politics. Mr. MAGGI!

ANGÉLICA: *[Looking at him sharply.]* We never get involved in those things!

[MAGGI nervously takes his pipe out of his mouth. In his nervousness, he turns the pipe upside down and all the tobacco falls on his jacket.]

MAGGI: But, what sort of politics are you talking to me about? *[He tries to clean off his jacket.]*

ANGÉLICA: *[Moving a piece.]* Didn't you say that the end of the party's broadcast upset you?

MAGGI: *[Very nervous. He moves the suitcase aside.]* I was never talking about politics!

PERLA: *[She sits down again and, as if nothing happened, resumes the game. To ANGÉLICA.]* Who was talking about it then?

ANGÉLICA: I don't know. I haven't the faintest idea.

PERLA: How strange. It seemed to me I heard talk of politics.

MAGGI: *[Putting tobacco in his pipe again, being very careful with what he says.]* No, what I said was that Sundays make me sad, when both parties leave the football field and the week's matches are over. *[Calmer now.]* It's the worst hour of the week.

ANGÉLICA: *[Pensively, in front of the table.]* Football parties?

PERLA: So you also play football? Check! *[The sisters continue playing. MAGGI, with his pipe in his mouth, makes gestures to indicate "no," but they are not looking.]* My father played on a football team for Standard Electric.

ANGÉLICA: So, where do you play?

MAGGI: *[Trying to light his pipe.]* No, I hear them.

ANGÉLICA: *[To PERLA.]* Speak louder because he can't hear.

PERLA: Is he deaf? Check!

ANGÉLICA: He said he couldn't hear.

MAGGI: *[With the pipe in his hand.]* Excuse me, but I don't understand...

PERLA: *[To ANGÉLICA.]* Talk louder, he doesn't understand you.

ANGÉLICA: *[To PERLA, vocalizing exaggeratedly, still playing.]* There is nothing to be ashamed of. Thirty percent of the population starts to go deaf at your age.

MAGGI: *[Standing up, very nervous.]* I was only saying that I don't play football. That I only listen to the games on the radio. *[He doesn't know what to do with the pipe in his hand.]*

PERLA: *[To Angelica.]* What does football have to do with deafness?

ANGÉLICA: [To PERLA.] Maybe he got kicked in his ear?

PERLA: *[To ANGÉLICA.]* Which one?

MAGGI: *[He touches his ear mechanically, realizes what he's doing, and brusquely drops his hand. He takes a few steps toward them.]* Let's get this straight, Ladies. I am not deaf! Nobody in my family is deaf! And I can hear the football games just fine, thank you!

[The pipe in his hand, due to his extreme nervousness, breaks.]
[MAGGI looks at the broken pipe. He tries to fix it, but he cannot. He puts the pieces in his pocket. He is disconcerted from the conversation between the sisters.]
ANGÉLICA: I read that in the United States there are special sports for the deaf.
PERLA: You'd better tell him that. *[Still playing.]* Check!
ANGÉLICA: I don't think he'd be interested, though. He's very unsociable.
[ANGÉLICA, though speaking to PERLA, is trying to get MAGGI'S attention.]
Very unsociable. *[Pause.]* Have you ever seen anyone more unsociable than Mr. MAGGI?
MAGGI: *[Reacting. He moves forward a few more steps.]* Ladies, you wouldn't happen to have a cigarette, would you?
ANGÉLICA: *[To PERLA, playing.]* Do you think he's all plugged up with wax?
PERLA: *[To ANGÉLICA.]* A good cleaning would unplug him.
MAGGI: *[Almost yelling.]* Ladies, would you happen to have a cigarette?
PERLA: *[Looking at him, astonished.]* Don't shout, we're not deaf!
ANGÉLICA: *[Getting up from the table.]* Nobody can play with such distractions.
MAGGI: *[Embarrassed, steps back.]* Excuse me, I didn't mean to bother you. *[He goes to the suitcase and picks it up. He heads toward the door.]*
ANGÉLICA: Mr. MAGGI. *[She sets up two chairs, facing each other, on either end of the table. MAGGI stops.]* Do you know what is the happiest memory from my childhood?
MAGGI: How's that, Miss?
[PERLA goes to the cabinet. She takes out a tablecloth and throws it over the table.]
ANGÉLICA: You're not going to believe it. Rainy Sundays! *[ANGÉLICA tell him all the following while PERLA sets the table with only two places. MAGGI*

remains still, listening to ANGÉLICA and, at the same time, watching closely to see if they are going to set a third place or not. PERLA stops periodically to serve herself another drink. After each sip, she stops briefly, as if dreaming. She caresses her medallion while murmuring something to herself. Then she returns to the table. In contrast, ANGÉLICA speaks and moves about very excitedly and quickly.] Do you know why? If, on Sunday, it threatened to rain, father wouldn't go to the tennis courts. He went to the courts every Sunday. But if it rained, he wouldn't go. He stayed home with us. On these days, we'd put on our best dresses. I had one red with white dots. It had ruffles on the sleeves. Everything had little white dots... white or gray, I could never tell. Father said I was his little princess. His adorable little princess, and that I had an aristocratic air about me. *[MAGGI slowly approaches the stool and sits down. There is a certain air of resignation in his attitude. His attention is divided between ANGÉLICA'S monologue and the table. He is visibly licking his lips.]* At noon, we took the bus and went downtown. The three of us, holding hands. We had lunch at the Fried Potato Palace. Cold cuts. The main course. And dessert. In the winter, we had soup. From there, we walked to the Royal Theatre, while father finished his cigar. They showed cartoons at the Royal. Movies with Chaplin, Laurel and Hardy, and... Shirley Temple! My idol! I always wanted to be like her. I imitated everything about her. I studied dance, singing, tap. I used to cry every night because my hair wasn't in curls. *[Pause.]* Finally, I got a perm. *[Pause.]* There were some movies that we'd watch four and five times in a row, since they kept showing them. And when we left the movies, if father was in a good mood, he'd take us to the candy shop to get hot chocolate, and sometimes he'd let us get seconds. *[Pause.]* Father always had a beer. They'd serve it to him in those really tall glasses, and I would taste the foam. *[Pause.]* What unforgettable days!

[The table is set for two people. PERLA sits down first and then ANGÉLICA sits down in front of her.]

MAGGI: *[Uncomfortable.]* I can imagine!
ANGÉLICA: *[Curtly.]* I don't think you can. They're memories, and memories don't interest anyone else.
PERLA: What did you do on Sundays?
MAGGI: On Sundays? *[The two sisters remain sitting at the table. MAGGI slowly regains his composure.]* I went to the cemetery.
PERLA: *[Alarmed.]* To the cemetery?
ANGÉLICA: What for?
MAGGI: To collect bones. *[He takes a cigarette out of his pocket and light it.]*
ANGÉLICA: What?
[PERLA nervously gulps down the contents of her glass.]
MAGGI: *[Very calm.]* Yes, to collect bones.
[The following monologue is given while he walks very slowly around the table with an attitude that says he is in total control of the situation.]
I made an arrangement with some medical students. They needed material for their classes and I went out and found them. During finals week they almost drove me crazy with all their requests. *[Pause.]* Later, I worked a lot with cadavers. *[He picks up a fork from the table.]* I sold them to the faculty. *[Pause.]* You know what the problem is. There aren't enough cadavers! They can't teach 50 students with only one cadaver. They need to have more. If not, what kind of doctors would they become? Without any real practice? *[Pause.]* They paid very well, you know. I arranged it directly with the school. It was good business! I worked in the Lincoln's neighborhood, from November to March. It's the best time. There are more accidents on the road. Some families would come to claim their deceased, but there were others who remained anonymous in the morgue that nobody came for. Those were the ones they cremated. We made a deal with the city and whenever there were unclaimed bodies down at the morgue, they would

call us. We went down there and loaded them up. We had a van. Some of them were very well preserved, you know? It was a good job. Quiet. Steady. *[Pause.]*

PERLA: But... why weren't they claimed... by anyone?

ANGÉLICA: Who were they?

MAGGI: Ah... vagrants, almost all of them. *[Pause. He is in front of them.]*

PERLA: You said, "almost all of them."

MAGGI: Yes. Why?

PERLA: And the ones who weren't vagrants?

MAGGI: Solitary people. People with no families. Lots of people die and nobody ever knows. *While he looks at them, he slowly twists the fork.* Old men, widows, pensioners. *[He looks sharply at them.]* Old maids. People without anybody. The most helpless ones. *[Long pause.]* You understand who I'm talking about?! *[ANGÉLICA and PERLA look at MAGGI. He appears transformed, with an attitude of superiority and, at the same time, menacing. With his right hand, he caresses his glove. PERLA and ANGÉLICA are terrified.]* The people most alone. The most helpless. You know, unprotected, defenseless. *[He faces them.]* People who don't even have a dog to bark for them! *[Pause. He stands the fork up, completely twisted, on the table.]* There are *a lot* of people like that. *[Pause.]* You know what I'm talking about, don't you?

[As he says this, MAGGI retreats to his suitcase. The sisters stand up. They are terrified. MAGGI picks up the suitcase. He sets it on the stool. He opens it and takes out something. PERLA and ANGÉLICA back away. MAGGI takes a small magician's table out of the suitcase. He sets it up quickly. He dresses it with a cloth. He takes out a top hat, then a wand. At no time does he look at the sisters. All his movements are those of a true magician. He does a few tricks very quickly. He plays with cards, Chinese boxes, scarves. The sisters go from terror to surprise. While they watch him, they return to their chairs and sit down. They are truly fascinated with what they are seeing, and evidently surprised. They look at

MAGGI. They look at each other. They laugh. MAGGI appears to be completely consumed by his role. He sets the top hat on the table. He makes one or two passes with the wand, lifts up the hat, and there is a small cage with a rat inside. At this moment, the sisters stop laughing. MAGGI lifts up the case. For an instant it is suspended. He dangles it. The sisters watch with fear and disgust. Slowly, MAGGI lowers the cage. He covers it with the hat. He taps the hat again, makes one or two passes with the wand, raises the hat, and the cage is gone. The sisters applaud, relieved, and at the same time surprised at the abilities of MAGGI. MAGGI bows very ceremoniously. The sisters continue applauding. As he bows for the third time, MAGGI grabs his sides, doubled over in pain.]

MAGGI: Arrgh! My hernia!

PERLA: *[Getting up from her chair.]* What's wrong?

ANGÉLICA: What is this? Another trick?

MAGGI: This is no damned trick! It's my herniated disc!

ANGÉLICA: *[To PERLA.]* His herniated what?

MAGGI: My disc, Madam, my disc! *[Talking to himself.]* Why did I bend over like that? As humid as it is! *[The sisters look at him, unsure of what to do.]* What are you looking at? Please help me! *[He takes a chair.]*

PERLA: Sure, why not? Do you want us to call an ambulance?

MAGGI: No, Miss. It's not that bad. Let's see. *[He motions to PERLA to come closer.]* If you please. *[He leans on her.]* Thank you. *[To ANGÉLICA.]* And you, please, start pushing me, a little at a time, so I don't have to make the effort. *[MAGGI, supported by PERLA and very bent over, begins to walk very slowly. ANGÉLICA pushes from behind. They go around the entire stage, until MAGGI looks up.]*

MAGGI: Where are we going?

ANGÉLICA: I don't know. You haven't told us.

MAGGI: *[Pointing to the sofa.]* Please... slowly... I can't take much more.

[The three go to the sofa. MAGGI sits down very carefully, supported by the two sisters. He continues to cry out in pain. He falls, almost lying down, on the sofa.]

PERLA: He looks like a baby.

ANGÉLICA: Don't you want a little pillow?

MAGGI: Thank you. You're very kind.

[ANGÉLICA puts a pillow under his head. There is a very maternal attitude about the sisters.]

PERLA: Well, you certainly can't leave here, in this condition.

MAGGI: This will pass in a moment and I'll be fine.

ANGÉLICA: You hope! We can't let you leave like this.

[ANGÉLICA begins to perfume herself.]

PERLA: Look if something happens to you. What an awful burden to bear!

MAGGI: I'm used to it.

ANGÉLICA: What, this always happens to you?

MAGGI: The vertebrae will fall into place in a moment and I'll be just fine.

PERLA: No, no. You're staying here.

ANGÉLICA: And we're not going to argue about it.

[PERLA goes to the cabinet. She pours herself a drink and drinks it. In her walk we can see a certain change from her former rigidity. She talks to herself. Her words are inaudible. ANGÉLICA turns on the radio. She sits down. She takes off her shoes. She picks up a magazine. A movie magazine. She reads while sucking her thumb. MAGGI, little by little, regains his composure. His expression is normal again. He looks at the sisters from the corner of his eye.]

MAGGI: Miss PERLA, would you be so kind as to bring me the stool?

PERLA: *[Quickly setting the glass down on the cabinet.]* Yes, of course. *[She brings it to him.]*

MAGGI: For my feet. Thank you. *[Pause.]* Miss ANGÉLICA, could you reach my cigarettes? They're in my jacket. *[ANGÉLICA turns off the radio and puts her shoes on quickly. She goes to his jacket pocket, takes out the cigarettes, and gives them to MAGGI.]* Thank you. A light! *[PERLA goes running to look for matches. She lights his cigarette.]* Whiskey! *[Each request is underscored by vigorous pointing with his right hand. ANGÉLICA looks for the whiskey bottle and a glass in the cabinet. She pours him a glass. She gives it to him.]* Ice cubes! *[PERLA brings him a bucket filled with ice cubes.]* Two! *[PERLA puts two cubes in his drink.]* One more! *[She adds one more. Pause.]* Cheese! Knife! Crackers! Napkins! Toothpicks! *[To each one of his requests, the sisters go running from one side of the room to the other, looking for things. With great excitement they anxiously await the next order.]* Newspaper! *[PERLA brings it to him.]* Radio! *[ANGÉLICA turns on the radio. A soap opera is on.]* Music! *[ANGÉLICA turns the dial until she finds music. MAGGI reads the newspaper while eating cheese and crackers and drinking whiskey. The sisters stay on their feet, waiting for new orders.]*

MAGGI: *[Without looking at them.]* You may leave now! *[PERLA and ANGÉLICA start walking towards the door.]* On your tiptoes!

[The sisters look at him. They look at each other. There is something of an unspoken agreement between them. MAGGI continues repeating "you are dismissed." He is seated comfortably. The two sisters suddenly begin throwing things at him: ice cubes, the plate of cheese, the magic props. He repeats, once more with greater force, "You are dismissed, don't you hear me? You are dismissed!"]

*[PERLA takes the suitcase and empties it on top of him. ANGÉLICA takes a shower cap and covers his face with it. With the things on top of him, the two sisters try to suffocate him. The scene is one of great violence and the two sisters seem to enjoy what they are doing to MAGGI. He twists about in his chair. Because his face is covered with the shower cap, it is difficult to hear what he is

saying, but he is obviously pleading with them to stop. *The two sisters are now practically on top of him, trying to suffocate him. With a great effort, MAGGI stands up. His head comes out from behind the shower cap far enough that he can see them. Everything falls to the floor. MAGGI'S attitude is menacing. He produces a cane from his clothing. The two sisters back away, going in different directions.]*

MAGGI: So you want to play rough, eh? Do you have any idea who you're playing with? Twenty five years slaving in the streets like a fool! So, you like to party? Well then, let's party!

[He bursts out in a hysterical laugh. He begins to strike the cane on the floor without looking at them.]

PERLA: *[Looking at MAGGI]* What's that?

ANGÉLICA: *[Frightened.]* PERLA!

PERLA: Mr. MAGGI, it was a joke.

ANGÉLICA: *[In a little girl's voice.]* Don't take it that way.

PERLA: Don't be upset.

ANGÉLICA: Of course he won't be upset.

[MAGGI moves towards them. He looks sharply at them. PERLA and ANGÉLICA back away, terrified.]

PERLA: Please, Mr. MAGGI. It's OK, now.

ANGÉLICA: *[To PERLA.]* Shut up! You're making him nervous!

PERLA: *[To ANGÉLICA.]* You shut up!

[MAGGI steadily looking at them and striking the ground with his cane, advances on them. His attitude is one of absolute coldness. The cane strikes closer to them each time. PERLA and ANGÉLICA are stuck together side by side. MAGGI'S cane strikes near PERLA'S feet. In the middle of the stage are the chairs the sisters used earlier to sit on. Terrified, PERLA jumps on top of the chair. MAGGI strikes at ANGÉLICA'S feet and she has no choice but to do the

same. The two are clutching the backs of the chairs. They look like circus animals. MAGGI is completely absorbed in his role, but he is moving with some difficulty, as if he cannot separate his feet when he walks. With one hand he gestures to them to stand up, with the other he holds the cane. The sisters obey him. During the entire scene, they cry out and sob. PERLA clutches hysterically at her medallion, and ANGÉLICA cries with her thumb in her mouth. MAGGI strikes the cane against the chairs and the sisters get down. He then directs them with the cane to change chairs, which they do--on all fours. Once the sisters have changed chairs, MAGGI takes a long pause. He begins to walk nervously, and with great difficulty. He trips over his suitcase and almost falls down. He immediately recovers and resumes striking at the legs of PERLA'S chair. The chair begins to shake, to the point of tipping over. PERLA, terrified, goes on all fours to ANGÉLICA'S chair and climbs up into it. PERLA and ANGÉLICA hug and comfort each other, but their faces are filled with terror. The whole scene has something of an erotic tint to it. MAGGI is hunched over and appears very uncomfortable and fidgety. His movements become more awkward and irregular. PERLA and ANGÉLICA sob uncontrollably. MAGGI directs them to turn around. They obey.]

MAGGI: Yes indeed, you've been bad little girls! Now your daddy has to spank your little bottoms! Isn't that right? Well then, let's see you pull down your little panties! Let's go! Let's go! Quickly! It's way past your bedtime. Let's go! Let's go! Hurry up!

[ANGÉLICA, trembling, begins to raise her skirt and lower her panties. PERLA, more reluctantly, does the same. The two cry and whine. MAGGI, who has been repeating the phrase "quickly," suddenly leaves the scene brusquely, but without making a sound. ANGÉLICA and PERLA, with their skirts raised and panties lowered, are still waiting for the blows of MAGGI'S cane. As the blows don't come, PERLA slowly turns her head and notices that MAGGI is not in the room.

In one swift movement she raises her panties, lowers her skirt, and jumps down from the chair. The crying of the sisters comes to an abrupt halt.]

PERLA: *[Letting go of ANGÉLICA.]* Mr. Miralles!

MAGGI: *[From offstage.]* I'm coming, Miss PERLA.

ANGÉLICA: What are you doing?

[ANGÉLICA gets down from the chair. She is furious. MAGGI appears. Now his stride is agile and sure. He looks at the expressions of the sisters and stops.]

ANGÉLICA: *[Violently.]* Do you want to tell me what you were doing?

MAGGI: I had to pee, Miss. I couldn't take it anymore.

PERLA: *[Indignant.]* And you had to choose just that moment!

ANGÉLICA: *[Picking up the cane and throwing it across the room.]* But, what were you thinking?

MAGGI: *[Surprised.]* But Miss, I've been holding it for an hour!

ANGÉLICA: Then you could have held it a little while longer!

PERLA: But, do you realize what you did?

MAGGI: *[Crushed.]* My bladder was bursting. I couldn't wait any longer!

ANGÉLICA: Come on, Mr. Miralles. You're not a little boy!

MAGGI: *[Conciliatory.]* If you'd like... we could start over.

PERLA: Don't be an idiot, OK?

ANGÉLICA: You've ruined our whole evening!

[The three look at each other. The air is filled with tension.]

MAGGI: Look, a thousand apologies, ladies. But some things just happen...

ANGÉLICA: Imbecile!

MAGGI: I don't have to take that!

ANGÉLICA: What don't you have to take?

PERLA: Let it go, Monica. He's not worth the effort.

MAGGI: *[Menacingly.]* You're going to regret...

ANGÉLICA: *[Ironically.]* Are you threatening me? *[ANGÉLICA and MAGGI stare hard at each other for an instant. Then ANGÉLICA turns to PERLA.]* You settle accounts. I don't want to talk to him anymore.

[ANGÉLICA goes over to a piece of furniture. From inside, she takes out a telephone. She begins to dial. Meanwhile, PERLA has found a pad and pencil. She goes toward Miralles. Miralles, meanwhile, takes off his coat and, with one hand, removes his moustache. His attitude is one of great weariness. The following dialogues occur simultaneously.]

PERLA: *[To MAGGI.]* Travel expenses?

MAGGI: 20 pesos. Here are the tickets.

[He takes the tickets out of his pocket, and gives them to PERLA.]

ANGÉLICA: *[Talking on the telephone.]* Hello... Hello, Rosita... yes, is the man of the house home? Thank you. *[To PERLA.]* Ask him for the list.

PERLA: Food?

MAGGI: A ham and cheese sandwich, a steak with a salad, and two coffees.

PERLA: Can't you eat something besides steak?

MAGGI: What am I supposed to do? I'm on a diet.

ANGÉLICA: Hello! How are you? Oh, I'm OK...

MAGGI: Three tonic waters.

ANGÉLICA: ... a terrible headache...

PERLA: Anything else?

MAGGI: The suit. Here's the receipt. *[He gives it to her.]*

ANGÉLICA: With whom...? You don't say!

MAGGI: The shoes are the same.

ANGÉLICA: How incredible! Always the same stupidity.

MAGGI: They're holding up well. It's the rubber soles.

PERLA: And what's all this?

MAGGI: The magic props.

ANGÉLICA: Yes, I'm with Silvia. She sends kisses.

PERLA: But they're not in the script.

MAGGI: No, but I thought you'd like them.

PERLA: Look, if you want to make changes, you have to let us know in advance. Let's see the list.

MAGGI: *[He takes out a list and reads.]* Four suitcases, six sets of undergarments...

ANGÉLICA: No, today's not good. If you'd like, we could do it tomorrow...

MAGGI: The parrot, the chess set, and the pipe. *[He continues reading.]*

ANGÉLICA: ...The one with Robert Redford...

MAGGI: All together... 250 pesos.

ANGÉLICA: Yes, that one...

PERLA: More than ten hours.

MAGGI: And eight hours.

PERLA: And eight hours of preparation... that's eighteen.

ANGÉLICA: Remember to call and confirm on Saturday.

PERLA: At 15 pesos per hour.

MAGGI: Excuse me, but last time, the lady *[He points to ANGÉLICA.]* told me 20. *[PERLA gestures to ANGÉLICA to consult with her.]*

ANGÉLICA: *[Covering up the receiver.]* I don't remember. *[She continues talking on the phone.]*

MAGGI: Come on, Madam, please. I'm tired!

ANGÉLICA: *[Covering the receiver again.]* Don't shout, this is not a tenement!

PERLA: *[Conciliatory.]* At 20 an hour, it comes to... *[Nervously making figures on the pad.]*

ANGÉLICA: Nothing, dear... What were you saying?

PERLA: It comes to 510. *[She gives him the pad.]* Check it over, if you like.

ANGÉLICA: Is there some young man over there?

MAGGI: Yes, it looks OK...

[He returns the pad to PERLA. She goes to a box. PERLA takes out a bundle of bills and gives it to Mr. MAGGI.]

ANGÉLICA: No, no, don't wait for me... Yes... around nine... *[PERLA whispers something to ANGÉLICA.]* Ah, tell Raul that Silvia is coming along this time...

PERLA: *[To MAGGI.]* Will you help me?

[The two of them begin to gather up all of the things on the floor, and put them in the suitcases, which now turn out to be four identical models.]

ANGÉLICA: Yes, yes... dear... of course. A big kiss. *[She hangs up.]*

[Pause. The three look at each other. ANGÉLICA, to MAGGI, conciliatory.]

ANGÉLICA: The part about the accident changed a lot, didn't it?

MAGGI: It was very long.

PERLA: I noticed you were a little distracted.

MAGGI: You know how it is. It's been a long day.

[The physical appearance of Miralles is the opposite of what it had been when he was MAGGI. His movements are slow, sure, and he no longer talks like a ruffian. Pause. The three, as if it were an old ritual, begin to take apart the room. Everything is a façade, nothing is real. They pile up the things in a corner. While they do this, one notes in the three of them movements crisp and violent, due to the tension among them. What remains on stage is an area that could be a house, or a garage, or a shack, etc. PERLA and ANGÉLICA, with a few changes, become a pair of high society ladies. MAGGI arranges his things and heads out into the hall. Before he leaves, he stops and turns around.]

MAGGI: Ah, I almost forgot to tell you. *[Pause.]* I have some new material. *[Pause.]* But, I don't know if you're going to be interested in it.

[Long pause. ANGÉLICA and PERLA look at each other. They look at MAGGI, and look at each other again.]

PERLA: *[Seemingly indifferent.]* What's it about?

MAGGI: It's about a drug addict. *[Pause.]* In New York. *[Pause.]* He breaks into the home of this family ... *[Pause. PERLA and ANGÉLICA return to what they had been doing.]* Are you interested? *[The sisters look at him without answering.]* Can I send you the scripts? *[The sisters resume their activities.]* Friday without fail. *[Pause.]* At two. *[Pause.]* Good afternoon, ladies. *[He heads toward the door. He stops.]* Ah, I forgot! *He takes out the black glove and gracefully leaves it on the table. He heads again toward the door.]*

ANGÉLICA: *[Authoritatively.]* Mr. Miralles!

MAGGI: Yes, Madam.

ANGÉLICA: I advise you to be on time!

MAGGI: *[Obsequiously.]* Yes, Madam.

PERLA: And do me the favor of wearing a clean shirt.

MAGGI: Yes, Madam, of course. Good afternoon.

[MAGGI closes the door stealthily. ANGÉLICA approaches a chair. She sits down. In front of her is a mirror. PERLA remains standing. She goes toward the glove. She takes it. ANGÉLICA looks at herself in the mirror. There is something of a tiredness, or defiance in her gaze. PERLA looks at her while stroking the glove. She raises the glove to her face. ANGÉLICA, in the mirror, is also watching PERLA. There is a long silence filled with gazes between the two women, in the mirror. Suddenly, PERLA brusquely hurls the glove at the mirror.]

Curtain.

That's All That

Sala Planeta, Buenos Aires (1981). In 1987 was performed at the Hispanic Theatre in Washington D.C., under the direction of Hugo Medrano, and in the Old Vic Theatre in London. The text was originally translated by Rodney Reading and Marta Avellaneda as *Over and Done With It*.

Acts

The cousin
The crush
The pad
The bachelor's party
An entire life

Characters

Skinny
The Brit
Finch
Fatso

A dim light illuminates the four actresses who slowly begin to change from their women's attire into children's clothes. Music accompanies this scene. Once they are dressed, the music quiets down and the light intensifies.

THE COUSIN

[SKINNY, FATSO and FINCH are seated on a park bench. The three are between the ages of twelve and thirteen. They are wearing faded ragged jeans, T-shirts, and tennis shoes. SKINNY takes aim with his water gun and shoots a pebble. FATSO is munching popcorn from a bag; he is always smiling. FINCH wears glasses and draws on the ground with a stick. FATSO looks to one side, pokes SKINNY in the ribs with his elbow. THE BRIT enters from where FATSO has been looking.]

SKINNY   Why are you lagging behind? *[Ironically.]* Did your mommy make you take a nap?

THE BRIT   Shut up, you asshole! Don't you know eat lunch late!

SKINNY   Oh, of course! Classy people never eat until three.

FATSO   That way they can skip dinner. That's why they're so well off.

[SKINNY and FATSO laugh].

THE BRIT   *[Upset.]* Tell them, Finch.

FINCH   What?

THE BRIT   Tell them how you stuff yourself when you eat at my house.

FINCH   How would I know? I don't keep track of how much we eat. But we ate for about two hours. I ended up with a belly like this big. *[He pretends he has an enormous stomach.]*

THE BRIT   Did you hear that, Skinny? It's not like at your house where they only fix you bologna sandwiches. *[Skinny seriously takes aim at him with his water gun.]* Stop! Stop it! What the heck are you doing? Aim at something else.

FATSO   *[Indicating an imaginary point with his head.]* Hey, Brit, look... here comes your girlfriend. *[The others laugh.]*

THE BRIT   *[Teasing him.]* Not quite, fat-ass. Look again, don't you know your own sister? *[Laughter. FATSO tries to hit him. THE BRIT dodges him.]*

FINCH   *[Indicating the same imaginary spot where the woman is standing.]* Hey, look! Her pants are so tight that if she takes a deep breath they'll rip.

THE BRIT   Yeah...*[to the boys]* Every time my sister has to put on her pants she asks my mom for help. It takes both of them to get the pants up over her hips. Then my sister lies on the bed and takes a deep breath. That's the signal for my mom to throw herself on top of her and zip them up. *[Pause.]* I call it Operation Zip-up.

FINCH   Hey, what does your sister do if she has to take a piss while she's out...does she call your mom?

SKINNY   What for? On the street she'd have a thousand guys waiting to throw themselves on top of her. Who needs your mom? *[Everybody laughs except THE BRIT. FATSO'S laughter is exaggerated. THE BRIT runs after SKINNY, but SKINNY escapes.]*

FINCH   *[Looking at the imaginary woman.]* Hey, look how she's trying to keep her balance. She can't even walk in those high heels. *[He imitates her.]*

FATSO   She's gonna bite it any minute.

THE BRIT Serves her right. Why does she wear them?

SKINNY   Come on! Your sister's got some. And hers look orthopedic!

THE BRIT Oh, come on! Your sister was in a cast for two months after she ran after a bus. Forgot already? *[A fight is brewing.]*

FATSO   *[Interrupting.]* That one dyes her hair.

FINCH   Look at this fat-ass, he thinks he knows everything.

FATSO   No, I don't understand shit....but my mom dyes her hair and it looks just like that.

SKINNY   Yeah, and there are a lot of weirdos out there who have rainbow-colored hair.

THE BRIT Can you imagine? Me...a redhead with hair down to my waist? *[He walks effeminately, playing the role of a homosexual].*

FATSO   And, me a blond with curls all the way down to my shoulders. *[A game of seduction begins between the two "fags". The other two play along, laughing excitedly. Every time FATSO passes by them, the others pinch his butt.]*

SKINNY   Hey fat-ass, you a chick...no way, man...not even the Boston Strangler would want you!

FATSO   *[In a high -pitched voice.]* Jealous!

SKINNY   Creep! [To the others.) Sure. Oh, that's it! I knew he reminded me of somebody. Look, he's just like his mom.

FATSO   *[Stopping the game.]* Stop talking about my mom. *[They're ready to fight again, but THE BRIT jumps in between them.]*

THE BRIT   Stop it, guys! Look what I got. *[He takes a magazine from underneath his shirt.]* I stole it from my brother. If he finds out, he'll kill me.

FATSO   Let me see! Show us!

SKINNY   Let me see!

FINCH   What's it called?

THE BRIT   It's a Playboy. In Swedish. *[All are bummed.]*

SKINNY   You moron, why didn't you bring one in Sanskrit?

THE BRIT   Don't be a dick. Don't you see it has pictures? *[They become enthused again.]*

FATSO   Cool! Pictures? Show us! Show us! *[The four of them fight over the magazine. They push each other. Whistle. Comment. Hottie! What a hottie!]*

SKINNY   Yeah, right. Now I know you're going to compare this babe with your mom...who is about forty and wears a wig.

FATSO   My mom doesn't wear a wig!

SKINNY   Oh, yeah? What fell off her head last week when she was out on the balcony watering the plants? Her brain?

[FATSO, furious, throws himself toward SKINNY. SKINNY ducks and FATSO falls, facedown, on the ground. They all laugh. SKINNY takes advantage of the position, grabbing his arm and twisting it behind his back. FATSO screams in pain.]

SKINNY   Say you're sorry!

FATSO   I'm sorry! I'm sorry!

SKINNY   Say, "I'm a fat asshole and a prick!"

FATSO   Hey, don't fuck around! *[SKINNY twists his arm harder.]* Okay, okay. I'm a fat asshole and a prick.

SKINNY   And a chicken.

FATSO   Okay, I'm a chicken! OW! I'm a chicken! *[SKINNY lets him go. FATSO stands rubbing his arm. He looks al SKINNY and under his breath says: "Dumbass."]*

SKINNY   What did you say?

FATSO   Nothing... Dum...That...

SKINNY   *[Pinching FATSO'S nose.]* Careful, fatty! Don't make me hurt you! *[He lets him go. When SKINNY turns around FATSO makes a series of obscene gestures at him.] [Pause.] [The four fool around awkwardly.]*

FINCH   There are guys who...dye their hair. "What a bunch of..." "Hey, look at these..." "What a piece of..."

SKINNY   Look at these babes! Where did they find them?

FATSO   Anybody can buy these magazines over there, right?

FINCH   Yeah, right... they even hand them out at school!

FATSO   No way! No wonder they're like that!

THE BRIT   What do you mean?

FATSO   They're all creeps.

FINCH   Who told you that?

FATSO   What! Don't you read the newspapers...don't you ever watch T.V.?

SKINNY   Look fat-ass, there are freaks everywhere... but girls like these!

FINCH   Hey Brit, what's it say here? Translate this part!

THE BRIT   Who wants to read? I just brought it so we could see the pictures.

FATSO   Can I tear out a page?

THE BRIT   Are you nuts? Can't you see that the pages are numbered? Hey, fatso, careful... watch it or I'll kill you!

FINCH   Hey, did I ever tell you guys about that time we were on vacation at my uncle's house and I saw my cousin...?

SKINNY   *[Shutting the magazine.]* What do you mean you saw her?

FINCH   Well... totally...naked.

FATSO   Wow, cool! Come on, tell us about it! *[They all quickly gather around FINCH.]*

FINCH   Well, one afternoon when it was really hot, everybody was taking a nap. I was in my room, real bored...so I went to the bathroom to get a drink of water...

FATSO   *[Making fun of FINCH.]* Yeah, right...to get a drink of water...*[He makes a gesture as if he were masturbating.]*

SKINNY   *[Hitting him on the head with the magazine.]* Shut up fat-ass!

FINCH   Well, I opened the bathroom door and there was my cousin...asleep in the bathtub.

THE BRIT   How old was she?

FINCH   Oh, about eighteen. I looked at her and then turned around to leave...then she called me.

FATSO   *[Imitating a female voice.]* FINCH! FINCH! *[They all laugh.]*

FINCH   I stopped at the door and my eyes were closed. Then...she asked me to keep her company.

ALL THREE No way!

SKINNY   You've got some cousin!

THE BRIT   Hey, how come you never introduced me to her before? Selfish bastard! From now on you're not going to see any more pictures.

FATSO   Go on, forget about them. *[SKINNY hits FATSO on the head again. FATSO screams. FINCH continues his story unperturbed.]*

FINCH   She told me not to open my eyes...that's what she said.

THE BRIT   Don't tell me you actually did it.

FATSO   *[To THE BRIT.]* He's not *that* stupid.

FINCH   At first I didn't open my eyes, then after a little bit, I opened them quickly, then closed them. Then I just kept them open the whole time...

SKINNY   What did she do?

FINCH   She talked to me. She said she was bored, that she was not allowed to go out. She was sick and tired of her family...I don't know. I wasn't listening.

FATSO   And...?

THE BRIT   Tell us! Hurry up!

FINCH   She asked me to wash her back. I played dumb. I took the soap and squeezed it so hard that flew up in the air and it fell into the bathtub...

FATSO   Doom—do—doom—doom!

FINCH   I tried looking for it. Without meaning to, I grabbed her leg. She jumped up and got me all wet. We couldn't get a hold of the soap. It slid around from one side to the other. We couldn't catch it! She laughed like crazy. She said I was tickling her. Just then the door opened and there was my aunt.

FATSO   Doom—do—doom—doom!

THE BRIT   Cut it out fat-ass!

SKINNY   Then what happened?

FINCH   The old lady took one step on the wet floor and fell on her ass. She started to yell, screaming all sorts of stuff at my cousin. The next day we left for home. The whole way home, my dad kept winking at me. My mom said that if I kept jerking off that up I'd end up being a dwarf.

FATSO   They tell me I'll end up crazy. *[Knowingly.]* Right, come on!

THE BRIT   Did you ever see her again?

FINCH   No, never. I think she got married... My mom said she was in a hurry to get married.

FATSO   Why was she in a hurry?

THE BRIT   What a retard! She was in a hurry...she was...you know.

SKINNY   Sure, every day her stomach got a little bigger... *[Everybody laughs, except FATSO, who looks confused.]*

FATSO   I don't get it, why are chicks always in such a hurry to get married... *[THE BRIT winks at SKINNY who is trying to contain his laughter]* ...if afterwards they bitch all day long. From the minute she wakes up, mom begins: "why did I marry this bastard...this jerk..." "I've ruined my life... I gave this imbecile my best years..." On and on and on....all day she gripes! *[Short pause.]* I don't get it... and then, if they don't get married, they go nuts...just like my aunt Rose, the poor old hag.

FINCH   Do you mean the one who wanders around naked in your yard?

FATSO   That's her... Now she's gotten even worse... She shits all over herself and doesn't even care.

THE BRIT   Why don't you lock her up?

FATSO   We don't have the dough, the nuthouse is expensive. My Dad says he isn't going to kill himself working all the time just so my crazy aunt can live like a princess...it's bad enough to take care of five drones.

THE BRIT   Five what?

FATSO   Drones...you know...the ones who... *[Makes an obscene gesture.]* bees. *[Everybody laughs.]* My Dad says she's going to bury all of us. Crazy people are tougher than steel... they live to be at least a hundred.

FINCH   Did you ever notice that there are more crazy women than men?

THE BRIT   Sure... I read in a book that chicks are much more screwed up than men, that's why they go crazy easier.

FINCH   Yeah, I heard they have one less gland than men.

SKINNY   What glands? They don't have any glands. They come with only half the parts. Look, last night my sister was at home with one of her friends. They kept looking in the mirror, and then she asked her friend, "Do you think I'm pigeon-toed?" Her friend said, "No way." Then she asked... "Tell me the truth, do I look better with or without bangs?" They were talking like that for three hours! Three hours! I could've killed them!

FATSO   What a bunch of fuck-ups.

SKINNY   *[Serious.]* Hey, blubber belly, don't mess with my sister. Got it? *[He threatens him.]*

FATSO   Hey, what's up? Are you on the rag again?

[Before SNINNY can react FATSO run and hides behind THE BRIT.] [Imitating what SKINNY said.] FINCH, tell me, do you think one leg is shorter than the other? *[As he says this he exaggerates a limp.]*

FINCH   *[Playing the game.]* No, not at all!

THE BRIT   So, tell me, how do I look best? *[He shows his profile.]* You like my profile? Or better like this? *[He turns front and his eyes are crossed.]*

FINCH   Yeah, just like that!

THE BRIT   Dressed... or naked? *[He begins a strip tease.]*

SKINNY   Man, you'd lose naked.

THE BRIT   Look who's talking, Tinker Bell.

SKINNY   Wanna bet?

FINCH   I'm in, whoever loses pays for the movies.

FATSO   Hey, stop! I don't got any cash.

SKINNY   Come on, fattyo! You've got to trust yourself.

FINCH   What if somebody comes by?

SKINNY   We'll just say... we had to pee all at once.

THE BRIT   Creeps! Wait until the chick looks the other way.

FATSO   Hey, the movies are too expensive. Don't fuck around.

SKINNY   Fatso, be a man once in your life. *[There is a moment of great expectation. The four look where the woman is supposed to be.]*

SKINNY   Okay, now!

[The four stand with their backs to the audience. They move their heads from

side to side. *They look at each other. They begin to laugh and titter. They all point at FATSO. They slap him, pull up their zippers, and then they turn around.]*

FATSO   I told you guys, I don't have any money.

THE BRIT   Don't make excuses...*[Ironically.]* Teenie... *[Laughter.]*

FATSO   Real smart! Let's bet to see who can eat the most jellybeans? Huh?

SKINNY   Don't be such a dead head fatso. Besides, when men speak, boys shut up.

THE BRIT   *[Indicating the imaginary woman.]* Look who she was waiting for.

FINCH   The ice-cream dude.

FATSO   *[Maliciously.]* She must be a real good cone-eater.

SKINNY   Wow, look at them making out... Hey, there're kids over here.

THE BRIT   Freaks! Can't you see there are children around? *[Points to FATSO.]*

FATSO   *[To THE BRIT.]* Hey, cut it out!

FINCH   Perverts! Child molesters! *[He covers his eyes.]*

FATSO   Hey, they're going. *[To THE BRIT]* Do you think they're gonna...

[THE BRIT looks at him with a self-satisfied glance. Everybody remains motionless, watching "The Couple" move away.]

SKINNY   *[Suddenly, breaking the ice.]* Hey, what's the matter? Wake up... You guys are jackasses today!

FATSO   *[Enthusiastically.]* Why don't we go key some cars? *[He takes out a key maybe from his pocket.]* There are three Mercedes around the corner... three!

FINCH   No, let's go scare the twin girls. I'll run home and get the frog.

THE BRIT   Stop screwing around with the girls. Let's go rip-off the newsstand, the one-eyed guy is there right now.

SKINNY   *[Taking aim with the water gun.]* The first one to get the old fart's hat gets a pack of cigarettes.

[No one says anything. Pause. They remain motionless staring forward. Suddenly, in unison, the four jump over the magazine left on the bench. The four, close together, begin to go through each page. Laughter, comments and pushing begin again. Slowly the sound and the lights fade out. Blackout.]

THE CRUSH

[A few props suggest that the scene takes place in a café. THE BRIT sits at the single table onstage. The actors in this scene are approximately seventeen to eighteen years old. THE BRIT is seated, reading a magazine. Every few seconds he nervously looks toward the entrance of the cafe. A love song is heard. After a short pause he raises his head and stares with a lost gaze for a short time. Suddenly he reacts to someone, "imaginary," who has entered the cafe. He smiles and timidly lowers his eyes back to the magazine. A light change could be made to indicate a more intimate atmosphere.]

THE BRIT   *[Speaking out loud to himself.]* Idiot, that's what you are, an idiot. You could have at least said hello to her. You've got to make a move. You've got to say hello to her, you've got to start somewhere. How are you going to invite her to the table if you don't look at her when she comes in. Besides, she's here alone. She never comes alone. So long, you lost your chance. Finito! Never again! Serves you right for being a dumb fuck. *[He cautiously looks in back of him where the "imaginary" woman is seated.]* You could ask her for a cigarette. *[Hitting his forehead.]* Yeah right, real original. You're a real loser!

Every day you turn into a bigger dumb fuck. How can you expect a girl to pay attention to you? Worst of all... she doesn't even smoke. No, not even that. *[Pause.]* Now, what can I do? She's not so friendly. That's for sure. I can't figure her out. Oh, shit... and now my stomach is growling. I wonder if she'll notice? Every time I get nervous my stomach growls. Okay, that's it! Just like during a test. Shut up, you idiot. It's not such a big deal. Okay, if she tells me to fuck off, well, I'm almost sure she will... Who knows? Maybe I'll... Might as well try". *[He turns around once again to see the girl meanwhile he ducks and twists to make sure she does not notice him.]* She won't look... To her, I'm the Invisible Man. *[He thumbs through the magazine without looking at it.]* What if I write her something? When I want to, I can write pretty well. It comes out better that way... I'll tell her that... that... *[He continues to thumb back and forth through the magazine, clearly nervous.]* No, it's better not to. Maybe she'll think I'm a moron and make fun of me with her friends. No, she wouldn't do something like that to me. Of course not. And what if she does? Huh? If she does, I'll die. I'll slit my wrists. *[He closes the magazine and then opens it again.]* I should have let my moustache grow out. I'd look older. I'm sure she doesn't like little boys. Tomorrow I'll bring a book by Norman Mailer. No, poetry, Rod McKuen, it's more romantic. No, Norman Mailer, it's more sophisticated, serious. Sure, maybe a good way to start things up. Tonight I'll do some reading, just in case... and I'll let my moustache grow out...starting today, I'll stop shaving. I'm gonna help Dad in his office to get some cash. The first date will be... it'll be to the theatre. Right, she won' t expect that. It'll completely blow her mind! What a genius! I'll let her go ahead of me everywhere. I'll open the door for her. Help her cross the street, I'll take her arm, then I'll let her go gently so she doesn't get the wrong impression. I'll keep asking her if everything is okay, if she's okay, if she wants something... That's it.

[While he is talking FATSO and SKINNY enter. A change of lighting here would switch off the intimate atmosphere. SKINNY is wearing dark shades. He is wearing a jacket, jeans, and boots. FATSO is also wearing a jacket and jeans, but everything on him is either too small or too big. They greet THE BRIT, clapping him on the back. They survey the situation with a provocative air. SKINNY sits down with the chair turned around [backwards], leaning over its back. FATSO imitates him. THE BRIT is sitting facing the audience. SKINNY AND FATSO are seated on the sides.]

SKINNY *[Grabbing the magazine from THE BRIT.]* What are you doing, dork? *[He throws the magazine on the table.]* *[FATSO takes the bottle of soda from THE BRIT and drinks it.]*

THE BRIT Hey, you're already starting with me!

FATSO Don't get pissed off, Brit, I'll get you another one later.

THE BRIT Yeah, right. You'll order another and drink that one too.

FATSO And who pays for it all?

THE BRIT Me!

FATSO *[Laughing.]* So, what's the matter? *[THE BRIT tries to hit FATSO, but FATSO pretends he doesn't know what's happening.]*

SKINNY *[Looking around the cafe, he speaks to THE BRIT.]* Did you check out that brunette behind you?

THE BRIT *[Pretending not to have noticed her.]* Which one? *[He turns around obviously.]* Oh, her?

SKINNY Yeah, do you know her?

THE BRIT No, I've never seen her before in my life. Why?

SKINNY No reason. *[Pause.]* She wants me.

THE BRIT *[Surprised.]* Who?

SKINNY The brunette.

THE BRIT How do you know?

SKINNY   She can't take her eyes off me.

THE BRIT   Are you sure? *[He looks straight at SKINNY who has a questioning look on his face.]* You know what? She's not that great.

FATSO   *[He is sprawled in his seat. He is biting his fingernails and spitting them on the floor.]* I'm telling you. She's a bitch. I always run into her at the bakery and she never says hello…doesn't even look at anyone.

SKINNY   Yeah, you can tell that she's kind of a prude. Look how she keeps her legs together. *[He imitates her.]*

[FATSO laughs loudly. THE BRIT also laughs, but forcefully.]

THE BRIT   *[To SKINNY.]* Look, I know these babes. The best thing you can do is not to pay any attention to them. That really drives them nuts.

SKINNY   *[Confidently.]* Look, I like it when they take a nibble…then good-bye. I leave them all hot and bothered.

[The three laugh. FATSO chokes and the other two slap him on the back. FINCH enters, says "hello," and sits down.]

FINCH   *[Excited.]* Hey, have you guys already heard?

THE THREE   About what?

FINCH   Don't you know anything?

THE THREE   No! What's up?

FINCH   Wow, it's an incredible mess.

THE THREE   Come on, tell us right now!

FINCH   It happened just around the corner. Looks like there was this chick, all dolled up, swinging her ass back and forth like a bell, back and forth, back and forth... then this old guy, little old guy…he was standing in line waiting for his pension check, said something to her, I don't know what... but this chick turns around and lets him have it with her purse.

FATSO   No way!

THE BRIT   Are you serious?

SKINNY   So... what happened?

FINCH   Well, the old guy broke his fall with his face...worst of all, his dentures fell out right there in the street. For the last fifteen minutes, and I'm not kidding...for fifteen minutes, everybody in the neighborhood has been helping him pick up his teeth. They even stopped traffic and a cop came over to see what happened. And that's not the half of it...when the other old guys saw the cop they asked him to take the girl away for being immoral... They said it was a public display of improper conduct.

THE THREE And then what?

FINCH   Well, I think they took her away.

THE BRIT   Good! Serves her right, damnit, first they tease you and then they act like they're innocent and pure.

SKINNY   If they dress that way it's only because they want to do it.

FATSO   Do you know where this one's gonna end up? In a whorehouse!

[FATSO laughs so loud that the others look at him as much embarrassed as amused.]

SKINNY   *[To FATSO.]* Since you're so chipper tonight, fatass, why don't you ask your pops for the truck and we'll go pick up some girls.

FATSO   Are you nuts? THE LAST TIME IT COSE OVER FIVE HUNDRED DOLLARS TO FIX IT. Since then he won't even talk to me.

SKINNY   Oh, man you're lucky!

FINCH   Yeah, lucky dog.

THE BRIT   Fatty, you're privileged. *[Laughing.]* You know what I did the other day? *[The others listen with expectation.]* I put up a little sign on my Dad's desk that said: "A father who gives advice is more than a father, he's a moron"... and what's even better is that I imitated my sister's handwriting. The old man was so pissed off that he went to my sister's room, grabbed her by the hair, threw her down on the floor and grounded her for a month. She can't even see her little boyfriend. *[They all laugh.]* You guys should have seen it! His face was so red because he was so mad and this vein right here was big and swollen like this *[Touching his forehead]*...and my retard of a sister wouldn't stop clucking like a hysterical chicken. What a sight! *[The three laugh loudly. SKINNY turns around.]*

FINCH   *[Turning around as well.]* Oh, that one, I know her. She lives around the corner from my house. She's got a thing going!

THE BRIT   What do you mean?

FINCH   A thing... a thing for the guys...always changing her clothes. A different one every day. I think she's a little...a little...

SKINNY   She gives it away!

THE BRIT   *[Unable to contain himself.]* Before you got here, she came over and asked me for a cigarette. *[He turns around obviously.]* As if I didn't know better!

SKINNY   *[With an expression of disgust.]* Don't bust my balls...that kind really gets me!

FATSO   *[To THE BRIT.]* So, did you try your luck?

THE BRIT   Are you nuts? Oh, yeah, right... after that who will get her off me?

[Laughter. The four begin to get more enthused. They move in toward each other.]

FINCH   Do you remember Laura? Laura...the one I had to tell that I had tuberculosis so she would stop bugging me?

SKINNY   And the way you look, she believed you right off the bat!

FINCH   Get off it!

FATSO   *[Rubbing his hands together.]* Hey guys, how about getting something to eat?

THE BRIT   Fatty, why don't you fuck off? You cost me more than a chick.

FATSO   Hey, what's the matter with you, are you on the rag again?
[Everybody laughs except THE BRIT.]
THE BRIT   Shut up! How long are you gonna keep on making the same stupid ass joke? *[On the sly he looks toward the girl. To FINCH.]* So...do you mean she's kinda...you know, kinda...
FINCH   What do you mean kinda? She's a real ho. The other day this old dude came to get her in this brand new car... You should have seen the old fart, he looked like a mummy.
FATSO   With these chicks you're dead without cash.
FINCH   Fatso...you're dead with or without cash.
SKINNY   But when they smell the dough...the panties come down.
[The four laugh. They scrape their chairs on the floor constantly switching places and positions on the chairs. They stand and then sit down. There is a feeling of great excitement.]
THE BRIT   *[To SKINNY.]*   You ever see Lulu anymore?
SKINNY   Are you nuts? Last time she wanted to jack up her fee and charge me out the ass. I just told her to go to go fuck herself. Besides, you have to put up with her kid crying all the time. She's all screwed up.
FATSO   I like Lulu. She's always smiling.
SKINNY   She's got a tick, you asshole! Somebody cut her up her face and left her mouth like this... *[He twists his mouth.]* You're a real dumb shit!
FATSO   Too bad, I really liked Lulu!
FINCH   *[To THE BRIT.]* Hey, how about the maid in your...house...did you already...
THE BRIT   Long time ago! Her second day on the job.
FINCH   Yeah? *Clapping him on the back.]* Horny bastard!
SKINNY   *[Self-assured.]* I know. You've got to get them right off the bat, then later it gets real tricky. You know, sure, no, maybe...sometime

soon...tomorrow...

FATSO   What do you know about that, Skinny? The only maid in your house is your mama. *[SKINNY pulls FATSO's seat out from under him, he falls to the floor.]*

THE BRIT   *[Upset, looking at the girl.]* Hey, you guys! Cut it out! Did you take some shithead pills today or what?

SKINNY   Hummm... It seems...It seems that your've got it bad for this chick.

THE BRIT   Are you high? Don't you know me at all?

SKINNY   You want me to ask her out?

THE BRIT   What for?

SKINNY   Just for fun. Wanna?

THE BRIT   I don't care... if you wanna...*[He shrugs his shoulders.]*

FATSO   *[Enthused.]* Come on, Skinny, turn on the charm.

SKINNY   *[Standing, in a gay boy voice.]* Should I?

FINCH   Sit down, you're making a fool of yourself.

SKINNY   Well sweetheart, where do you think you are? At the Plaza?

FATSO   Look! Look! She's getting nervous.

THE BRIT   *[Carefully turning around.]* Skinny, do whatever you want. But it's just a waste of time. She's not worth it.

FINCH   *[To SKINNY.]* On a scale of one to ten...

SKINNY   Out of ten... I'd give her four or five. Just cause of those hooters. *[He indicates enormous breasts with his hands.]*

FATSO   Yeah...and then she looks at you with that screwed-up wandering eye.

FINCH   Don't lie, Fatty. She wouldn't waste her time on pachyderms.

[FATSO shrugs his shoulders. He takes an enormous chocolate bar from his pocket and begins to eat it.]

SKINNY   She's paying her check!

FATSO   What do we do now?

THE BRIT   Just get her when she leaves.

SKINNY   You think so?

THE BRIT   If you feel up to it...

SKINNY   You think so? *[He stands and then sits again. Pause.]* Nah. Better not. Let's do it some other time. *[Self-assured.]* I'm not up for it today... You know how these things work. A lot of talk...a lot of bullshit.

THE BRIT   *[Relieved.]* You're telling me.

FATSO   *[Laughing and spitting the chocolate.]* Look, she's the same size standing as sitting.

FINCH   Just like Miss FATSO?

[THE FOUR of them laugh loudly. THE BRIT forces himself to laugh. By the look of the four boys, we can tell that the girl is passing them on her way to the exit. The following happens at a very rapid pace.]

SKINNY   *[To the girl, licentiously.]* Don't look at me like that, you'll blind me.

FINCH   *[To the girl.]* Switch to your low beams, please, or we'll crash.

THE BRIT   *[To the girl, but first looking at the other boys with an air of complicity.]* If you say no, I'll slit my wrists. *[He winks at the others, they don't stop laughing.]*

FATSO   *[Offering the girl chocolate.]* It's on the house. No strings attached. Let me see that little mouth.

[From the boys gaze it we realize that the girl has already passed them by and is standing with her back to them. FATSO makes a spit wad with the paper from the chocolate and throws it at the girl.]

FATSO   Who do you think you are? Midget!

[The girl has left and the four return to the table.]

SKINNY   *[Looking at the others.]* Fuck off, you skinny bitch!

FATSO   Did you see that? Her... *[pointing at his buttocks]* is sagging. What did I tell you?

FINCH   No wonder she goes out with old guys.

THE BRIT   Who does she think she is?

[Pause. All four still maintain an air of excitement. They look at each other. They smile. They slap each other on the back. They make rapid and nervous movements that slowly come to a stop. The ambiance slows down. They look at each other. They check the place out. Silence.]

SKINNY   *[Standing.]* I'm going to the club. It's like a funeral in here. *[To FATSO]* Are you coming?

FATSO   I can't. They're waiting for me at home for dinner.

[FINCH and SKINNY pretend to vomit. FATSO flips the bird. He stands with great difficulty and slowly picks up things from the table. SKINNY looks at FINCH.]

FINCH   I promised the hag to help her kill cockroaches. When I woke up this morning there was one on my pillow, staring right at me.

THE BRIT   *[Disgusted.]* ......Ugh!

SKINNY   *[Playfully.]* What did you do?

FINCH   Nothing. I asked him to forgive me for snoring and went back to sleep.

[SKINNY lightly taps FINCH. They both stand and go to the exit.]

SKINNY   *[To THE BRIT.]* Come out for a while. We'll find something for sure.

THE BRIT   Maybe later.

[He opens the magazine and pretends to read. When he sees that the others have left, he slowly turns around. He remains that way for a few moments. As if

remembering something, he slowly strokes an imaginary moustache and takes a deep breath. He takes money out of his pocket. All of his movements are very measured. He leaves the money on the table. He stands and turns to look once again at the table where the girl was seated. He turns around and picks up the magazine. He signals to the people in the bar with the magazine, without looking at them. Then he leaves the stage slowly.]

THE BACHELOR'S PARTY

[FATSO, FINCH, SKINNY, and THE BRIT are seated facing the audience. They are between thirty and thirty-two years old. The four are wearing jackets. THE BRIT wears an elegant suit. SKINNY has combed his hair back with hair gel. He has a moustache. His tie is brightly colored and he wears a large flower in his buttonhole. FINCH is the only one not wearing a tie, is wearing a turtleneck. There is something ambiguous about him. FATSO wears a very tight shirt, a thin tie, and extremely long sideburns. In front of them there is a mountain of dirty dishes and half-empty wine bottles. At the beginning of the scene it is difficult to understand the dialogue because they are speaking animatedly. They laugh and drink. The ambiance is festive. After a while THE BRIT stands, with a glass in hand, and begins to speak. This time he is understood.]

THE BRIT   *[To SKINNY.]* Today, to our buddy who leaves us to join the legion of the... *[With his hand he makes the sign of a "cuckold." [He sits. They all laugh. SKINNY serves wine to everyone.]*
FINCH   *[To SKINNY.]* Did you get a raise because of the wedding?
SKINNY   Yeah, they gave me some cash... they outdid themselves... I don't even have enough dough to pay for the wedding cake.

FATSO   Then just have a party with doughnuts...what are you gonna do?

SKINNY   As soon as I save a couple of bucks, I'll quit. I'll open a little shop or? whatever... and see ya!. *[He flips the bird.]*

TILE BRIT   Are you nuts?...now that you're getting married you're thinking of saving?

SKINNY   Yeah...why?

THE BRIT   Don't you know that with a woman in the house there's never enough money? You'll see...

SKINNY   She tells me she wants to get a job...but I won't let her just now.

FATSO   You're right. If they get out of the house to work, then they soon start giving you reheated scraps and canned food.

SKINNY   I already told her that as long as I have two good arms, I'm the one who brings home the bacon.

FATSO   Damn right!

FINCH   So, what did she say?

SKINNY   Nothing. What could she say? Do they want to know who wears the pants or not?

FATSO   Right, that's the way most chicks are, but not my mother. The other day I told her I wouldn't water the plants and she threw a shoe at me. Wanna see? I still got the bump.

THE BRIT   I opened Sylvia a boutique.

SKINNY   A boutique?

FATSO   What for?

THE BRIT   To keep her busy.

SKINNY   Why?

THE BRIT   She said she was bored at home. Being locked up all day long with the kids makes her nervous.

SKINNY   I'd kill her.

FATSO   So why did she have kids if they make her nervous?
FINCH   Maybe she wants to get out…to do other things.
SKINNY   Ever since you got into psychology you're acting kinda weird.
THE BRIT   To tell you the truth, I opened the boutique for her so she'd stop nagging me.
SKINNY   That's more like it.
FATSO   He's not such a dumb prick.
FINCH   *[To SKINNY.]* So…you think I'm a freak?
SKINNY   What's up with you? Are you fucked up?
FINCH   No, I was just asking.
SKINNY   No, Billy, you're a heck of a guy. A great guy. *[To THE BRIT.]* Hey, let's hear it, maybe we'll learn something.
THE BRIT   Well, you all know Sylvia.
SKINNY   *[Licentiously.]* Up one side and down the other.
FATSO   Yeah, we were joined at the hip!
THE BRIT   *[Serious.]* Do you want me to tell? Yes or no?
SKINNY   Yeah, dude, tell us!
THE BRIT   Sylvia has always been very jealous… *[SKINNY reinterprets with a mocking gesture, THE BRIT looks straight at him and SKINNY pretends not to know what he means while FATSO laughs hilariously.]* When she was at home she'd control everything I did. She used to call me at the office three or four times a day, just to control me. So when she told me she was getting bored, I gave it a thought, then I set up the boutique for her. Now she's there all day long. It keeps her entertained, she hangs out with her friends, and she brings home a little cash, that never hurts… and as the store is right downtown in the center of the shopping area, so she's so busy that she doesn't have the time to eat and even less time to call me Kaput!
FATSO   Ka—what?

SKINNY   That's it! She's screwed!

THE BRIT   She's happier and I'm as free as a bird.

FATSO   Clever bastard!

SKINNY   Cool! So what? Look, you get married and bust your balls trying to feed them, the least you deserve is to be able to chill out, no?

FINCH   Yeah, right, Skinny, we all know you were anxious to set a date.

SKINNY   What do you mean I was anxious? Are you crazy? Are you drunk already?

FINCH   Look, don't pretend to be such a pompous ass. Everybody in the neighborhood knew about Susie and Shortie.

SKINNY   *[Very upset.]* Are you nuts or something? Shortie is like family. He's like a brother.

FATSO   Sure, a brother who almost stole your girl.

SKINNY   Shut up fatso, it's none of your business.

FINCH   Isn't it true that Susie asked you to give her a break? Said she wanted to think it over?

SKINNY   So what? You gotta think these things through.

FINCH   After six years of engagement?

SKINNY   *[Disconcerted.]* Right... *[Recovering.]* What are you trying to do? Fuck up my party?

FINCH   No, dude! After all, she's marrying you, isn't she?

SKINNY   Yeap! Of course...she's gonna marry me!

FATSO   *[Standing with the glass in his hand.]* To Skinny! Whom in hand to hand combat with Shortie Beckwith... finally scored some points by speeding up the deal to become the happy champion of the fu...

SKINNY   *[Seats him with a push.]* Careful with what you say fatso. If I start talking...

FATSO   *[Waving his hands.]* Oooh!...I'm so afraid of you, man!

THE BRIT   *[Looking at FATSO and FINCH.]* Well, it's down to you two.

FATSO   I'll never get married!   No way! After putting up with my mother, I don't wanna know a thing about living with women. *[Pause.]* When I want some, I pay for it and that's that. Over and done with it!

FINCH   But, you never fell for anybody?

FATSO   Well, yeah... but the ones I like don't pay attention to me. What do you want me to do? Tie it in a knot?

THE BRIT   No, just quit eating like a pig.

FATSO   Why? If I like eating more than picking up chicks...

SKINNY   Tell me fatty... what do you feel in the dark when you tenderly caress yourself with a chicken leg?

[FATSO is about to throw a piece of bread at him. SKINNY stares back at him. A fight is about to begin. THE BRIT breaks it up.]

THE BRIT   And you FINCH? What are you up to? Sitting there so quiet?

FINCH   Just chilling out.

SKINNY   *[In an altered voice.]* We may not be manly...but we are many!

[Everyone laughs except FINCH.]

FINCH   Look, you better hurry up and sign your name on the dotted line... I can already see you out there roaming the streets.

SKINNY   It was just a joke, FINCH. I know you work hard.

FATSO   Yeah, working his wrist *[They all laugh. FINCH smiles.]*

SKINNY   *[Raising his glass.]* Guys! For them!... The beauties... *[They all drain their glasses.]*

SKINNY   *[To THE BRIT.]* Hey, how about Monica, you still dating her?

THE BRIT   Every Tuesday, between seven and nine...

SKINNY   And what do you tell your wife?

THE BRIT   A Board of Directors meeting. Weekly reports. They already know at work. They just turn on the answering machine.

SKINNY   I'm going to have to make something up. Maybe I'll use you, fatty. But don't fuck it up.

FATSO   Leave everything written out for me, cause if I'm pressed for information, I get nervous and sing like a canary.

SKINNY   If you sing, I'll wring your neck like a bird. Useless jerk!

THE BRIT   Do you remember Chimp? Chimp Anderson? A good friend of mine.

SKINNY   Which one? The guy who always dressed so well except in winter when he used to wear sandals with wool socks?

THE BRIT   Yep, that one! I bet you can't imagine what happened to him.

FATSO   Someone stole his socks!

[THE BRIT hits FATSO on the head.]

FINCH   Sure, I remember him, he was kinda of a creep. What happened to him?

THE BRIT   Well, every time he had a fling, he'd tell his wife that he was at the gym. At the gym, the manager knew everything and when the wife called he'd always say: "Yes ma'am, he was here a moment ago but he just went to the showers." Or, "He just went to the dressing room, would you like to leave a message?" Then Chimp would call the club later and they'd bring him up to date. *[Short pause.]* One day, when they really were waiting for him for a tennis match, he was at home, not feeling too well. He asked his wife to call the gym and tell them that he wasn't coming in. His wife dialed and the guy answered, when she said "this is Mrs. Anderson," the guy starts blabbing, "How are you?... What a coincidence! Your husband just passed by on his way to the showers. Would you like me to give him a message?" *[The four laugh.]* Can you imagine what a shower that must have been! Wow!

FATSO   So, what happened?

THE BRIT   The joke cost him a trip to the islands, he had to redecorate the whole house and give up his membership to the gym.

SKINNY   What's he doing now?

THE BRIT Now he says he's going to Alcoholics Anonymous.

FINCH   What for?

THE BRIT He's hooked up with an alcoholic. *[The four laugh harder. They continue to drink. It appears to be a real binge. They continue. Then they break.]*

FINCH   Hey, you know I'm moving?

SKINNY   Great! Where to? The Lonely Hearts Club? *[They all laugh.]*

FINCH   I rented an apartment downtown…not too far from work.

THE BRIT *[Self-assured.]* How much are you paying a month? I'll tell you if they fucked you over.

FINCH   To tell you the truth I'm sharing the rent.

FATSO   Really? So you finally fell for somebody.

SKINNY   That's great FINCH.

THE BRIT What's she like…is she a real man-eater?

FINCH   No…You didn't let me finish. I share it…with this other dude. It's this guy who needed extra money and offered it to me. I saw it advertised in the newspaper. But the apartment is huge, so it's not…

[The three are disconcerted.]

SKINNY   Hey, this sounds a little fishy, if you ask me.

FATSO   *[Hitting a glass on the table.]* First he wants money then he'll want a little action.

FINCH   Don't be a prick. He's a great guy. An artist.

THE BR1T So what are you, the model?

SKINNY   Come on, FINCH, tell us… What's it feel like?"

FATSO   Is it for real? Or are you fooling around?

THE BRIT FINCH…

FINCH   What?

THE BRIT   *[Feigning concern.]* I hope you're on the pill. *[FINCH loses control and throws the contents of his glass in his face. THE BRIT stands, hysterical.]* My suit, it's made out of English wool! You didn't have any right to do that! Don't you fuck with me!

[FINCH gets up to leave. SKINNY signals to FATSO. The two stand. SKINNY grabs FINCH from behind. FATSO helps. Between the two of them they force him on to the table, face down. It's obvious that they have all been drinking too much.]

THE BRIT   *[He continues to wipe himself off.]* Hey, what the hell are you doing? Stop! Everybody's watching.

SKINNY   Confess it, FINCH. Tell us you've gone that way...

FATSO   What do they call you now? Queenie?

SKINNY   Do you dress up like a chick? Tell us! Do you dress like a chick?

FINCH   Let me go, shit! Let me go! You fuckers! *[FATSO throws the rest of his dinner on FINCH'S head.]*

THE BRIT   *[Uncomfortable.]* Stop it! Cut it out! People are laughing! This spot won't go away, English wool! I've only worn it twice. Only twice!

SKINNY   *[Uncontrolled.]* Do you wear make-up FINCH? Tell us! Do you put on lipstick! Come on, tell!

FATSO   Do you wear panties? Little white panties? Huh? Tell us! *[The two stand in back of FINCH. There is something very abusive about the scene.]*

SKINNY   How about pantyhose! And high heels?

FINCH   *[Weakly.]* Stop fucking around... Let me go. Bastards...

FATSO   Don't be shy FINCH. Tell us! We're your friends. What are friends for, right, Skinny?

[THE BRIT is very upset and he speaks to them with his voice lowered. He tries to signal them to "cut it out, stop!" The two don't acknowledge him and they

appear to be excited by the game.]

SKINNY   Do you wear lipstick?

FATSO   Do you dress like a chick?

SKINNY   Bright red lipstick?

FATSO   White panties?

SKINNY   What's the matter, bitch? Say something!

FATSO   Don't be naughty, tell us!

SKINNY   So where do you pick up guys, in the bathrooms?

FATSO   In the train stations?

SKINNY   Do you like old guys?

FATSO   Or boys?

SKINNY   Do you use a bra? Huh?

FATSO   And matching panties?

FINCH   *[Almost crying, in a loud voice.]* No assholes! I'm gay, but I'm not a woman! Do you understand? You fuckers! I'm gay but I'm not a woman! You fucking bastards!

[They are disconcerted. SKINNY and FATSO slowly let FINCH go. Long pause. SKINNY smiles. THE BRIT and FATSO also smile. Without looking at them FINCH begins to composes himself.]

SKINNY   *[As if nothing has happened. Slapping FINCH on the back in "friendship."]* This FINCH, shit!

THE BRIT *[Helping to clean him off.]* You guys go overboard. You get carried away and act like real assholes... just like when you were kids.

FATSO   Don't get so mad, man. It was just a joke. Today it was your turn... tomorrow it will be my turn. That's life. Right?

[FINCH continues to clean himself off slowly, he doesn't look at them.]
[Pause.]

SKINNY   *[Carefully.]* Isn't FINCH great? He can't take a joke.

THE BRIT   *[Playing along.]* He could sell you the Brooklyn Bridge.
FATSO   He always gets you!
SKINNY   Do you remember the time he made us believe that he had polio?
THE BRIT   Yeah, and I gave him my favorite electric train.
FATSO   Remember that day at the pool when he screamed he had a cramp?
SKINNY   I jumped in to save him. I nearly drowned for real.
FATSO   No wonder, the shoes you were wearing weighed twenty pounds a piece.
THE BRIT   *[Affectionately.]* He's a son of a bitch!
SKINNY   With that angel face? Who would have thought it?
[THE FOUR embrace. SKINNY takes a glass from the table and proposes a toast.] To us! To our friendship!
THE BRIT   *[Very drunk.]* May a chick... no matter how stacked... not matter what kind of chick she might be... come between our friendship.
SKINNY   Like real men!
FATSO   Damn right!
SKINNY   Here's to the good times!
ALL   Bottoms up!
[The four embrace with their glasses raised begin to sing facing the audience.]

THE PAD

[A few props suggest the living of a one-bedroom apartment]. The apartment lacks any decoration. Everything is impersonal. THE BRIT and SKINNY are seated, each has a glass of whiskey in his hand. FINCH, standing, pours a drink. A flush is heard from the bathroom. From one side FATSO enters. All are dressed in summer clothes. They are between forty-three and forty-five years

old.]

SKINNY *[To everyone, indicating the apartment.]* So, how do you like it?

THE BRIT It's okay... just the right price...

FINCH Did it come furnished?

SKINNY Sure, it's a lot less trouble.

FATSO What about the kitchen? Don't you have a kitchen?

SKINNY It's a kitchenette. But you ought to know by now fattyo' that I don't do much cooking around here. *[Laughter.]*

THE BRIT *[To SKINNY.]* What time did you tell them to come?

SKINNY There's still time. They don't get off till twelve.

THE BRIT Hey, fatty, give me another whiskey.

FATSO *[While serving the drink.]* What about the movies? Did you bring the movies?

SKINNY Yeap! But we're going to wait for the chicks to get here before we show them.

FATSO How about the magazines?

SKINNY Look fatso, I've got everything under control. Chill, okay?

FINCH *[To FATSO.]* Hey, what's the matter with you? How long has it been since you've...

FATSO *[He makes such a quick gesture that he nearly knocks everything over.]* How can I get any if I'm always playing nurse. Mom just keeps getting worse. *[He takes the whiskey to THE BRIT.]* Now it's her kidneys, before she had bronchitis, and before that hemorroi...

THE BRIT *[Interrupting.]* Look fatso, you don't have to go into details.

FATSO *[Carried away with himself.]* Okay, but every cent I make goes to get her medicine. Besides, she won't let me go out at night, so she won't be alone. She says that she hasn't put up with me for forty years to die like some old dog, all alone. What do you want me to do? She's my mother!

SKINNY   So what happened today fatty? Are you playing hooky?

THE BRIT   I'm sure he drugged her.

FINCH   So what did you invent this time porky?

[Pause. Everyone looks at FATSO.]

SKINNY   So, what did you tell her?

FATSO   That... that FINCH was introducing us his fiancée to all of us tonight. She got so choked up that she nearly came with me. *[Pause. They all force a laugh. THE BRIT stands.]*

THE BRIT   Skinny, don't you have any music?

SKINNY   Sure man, over there there's a little of everything. *[SKINNY puts a record on the record player. FATSO practices a few dance steps, followed by laughter as they urge him on. SKINNY turns the music down so low that it is barely audible.]* The neighbors are a bunch of... *[He makes the gesture of being crazy.]* Should I tell you the latest? They complained that the bed made too much noise, they couldn't sleep.

FINCH   Come on! What did you do?

SKINNY   Nothing. What do you want me to do? Maybe I could oil the mattress. *[Laughter.]* They're driving me crazy. The other day I was right in the middle of doing it when they started banging on the ceiling with a broom handle. You can imagine, kaput!

FATSO   Ka—what?

THE BRIT   Fatso, when are you going to stop asking the same thing? Kaput! It stopped functioning, that he lost in the middle of the war. *[He indicates with his index finger.]* Now do you get it?

FATSO   Oh, right! If you make yourself clear, of course I get it. *[Pause. Seriously.]* Look, Skinny, I've got some advice for you. I'd just pick up my things and move. If every time you jump in the sack they're going to stop you, you're going to end up... Got it?

SKINNY   Are you insane, fatty? You know how much it cost me to get this place, all the extra time I put into it! The sacrifice. You're nuts! I'd rather put a mattress in the bathroom than move out of here. Not on your life!

THE BRIT   *[Pointing at the floor.]* Don't get upset, they're just jealous.

SKINNY   Sure, I know that. Every time the doorman sees me come in with somebody new he gets green with envy. One of these days he's going to swallow his duster out of envy. *[Laughter. Pause.]*

THE BRIT   Hey, you guys, did I tell you that my little Lisa has a boyfriend?

FATSO   Who? Your kid?

FINCH   Man... Already? How old is she?

THE BRIT   Seventeen. She's still a kid.

SKINNY   Yeah, but with that body she's got... she's a real hottie! *[He outlines a curvaceous body with his hands.]*

THE BRIT   *[Upset.]* Yeah, but she's just a kid. *[He touches his head.]* She's still a kid up here.

FINCH   So, who is he?

THE BRIT   A real bum... a loser! He's studying theatre, and worse than that, in his free time he's a poet. *[The three laugh.]*

FATSO   Oh, no! That sucks, Brit!

FINCH   That's all you need, a poet.

SKINNY   So what are you going to do? I suppose you have to do something?

THE BRIT   Sure. I sent her away with her mother for the summer. I rented a house in Cape Cod. I hope she'll forget about him or find somebody better. They're real green at this age. *[Short pause.]* You know what I mean? You bust your balls giving them everything so they won't be without anything, then along comes the first asshole and takes her away.

FATSO   That's not fair!

SKINNY   You know what it is, Brit, nowadays kids are messed up. Look at girls today, they don't care about anything... They all give it away.

FINCH   *[To THE BRIT.]* And what would you do if you found out that your daughter was no longer a... well... you know...

THE BRIT   *[In fatherly tone.]* My kid? *[Quickly changing his tone.]* I'd kick her out of the house. No doubt about it. If she wants to live her own life, let her live it. But not at my expense. Especially with this useless bum. Come on! *[Pause.]* Poetry my ass! You remember when we were his age? Nothing got by us! We acted like real men! Ain't I right?

FINCH   Times change. They're not so formal, now everything is more direct.

THE BRIT   Right, you talk like that, 'cause you don't have children.

SKINNY   Thank god my daughters are still playing house. I'll sleep okay for the next few years.

FATSO   *[To SKINNY.]* So when's the boy coming?

SKINNY   If not in February, we'll keep trying. We're still looking for him. But until he comes, I won't stop. I already told my wife that.

THE BRIT   You're right. Women are really complicated. Too much crap in their heads, as if men didn't have enough problems...

FATSO   *[To THE BRIT.]* Hey, speaking of problems... thanks for the address... you really saved my ass!

THE BRIT   Why? Was it getting complicated?

FATSO   You can only imagine, she was already three months along.

THE BRIT   Did everything turn out okay?

FATSO   How should I know? I gave her the address and a few hundred bucks... I didn't see her again... who knows if...

SKINNY   Sounds okay! The chicks today all pretend to be independent, but the minute things get fucked up, then they want a guy to protect them. It's easy to live that way, right?

FATSO   That's what I always say.

SKINNY   *[Standing.]* Hey, fatty, come with me, let's go buy a couple of pizzas.

THE BRIT   Hey, while you're out... *[To FINCH.]* These chicks soak it up like sponges. They're all the same. *[SKINNY and FATSO exit. THE BRIT and FINCH remain, face to face. Long pause.]*

THE BRIT   How's life treating you? How're things going?

FINCH   Oh, you know, breaking my back like always, but I can't complain.

THE BRIT   I'm glad. I'm happy for you. You want another whiskey? *[FINCH nods and THE BRIT serves him.]* That's great, that's really great. *[Pause.]* Great. *[Pause.]* You know... I don't like to stick my nose into somebody else's affairs. You know me. It's not my business, if it were up to me everybody could live the way they wanted. To each his own... But you know, I've been thinking... You're a good friend. We've known each other for a long time, since we were kids. Wow! Maybe thirty years... all our lives. You have your story and I have mine. Would you like a little more ice? *[FINCH holds out his glass and THE BRIT serves him ice.]* You know, FINCH, I think, and I don't want to get involved in anybody else's affairs, but you ought to go out with a chick. Yeah, I already know, you don't have to say anything... I'm only saying that you ought to go out, well, so you can be seen, you know, so they can see you... get it? Just for appearances. You know, go out. Go to the movies. Walk down the street. On Sunday go to the park. Do you understand me? Catch my drift? You'll be seen. They'll see you. So others see you, out, with a real looker. You know, arm in arm. Understand? FINCH? *[Pause.]* Well, if you don't... you know how people like to talk... I know, who cares what everybody else says? *[Getting closer.]* Look, I'm your friend, Skinny's your friend, FATSO... they always see us together. People talk. They come to their own conclusions. And then what? Suppose they decide that all of us are, well you know, alike? Hey! Don't get me wrong! It's not because of me. I'm your friend. It's because of the family, you know. I have sons. Daughters. There are certain values, customs. I wouldn't like it if tomorrow one of my sons came to tell me that... well, you know what I mean. You know what life is like. FINCH? It's not easy. Not for you. Not for me. Why let them talk? Huh, why? Damnit, if there're more than enough chicks to go around. There're enough of every kind. I could introduce you to some if you wanted. You could go out a bit. Show them off. They'll see you. You could rub it in the assholes' faces. Bang! Everybody would be happy then! *[Moving away from him.]* If I were you I'd give it a try. What have you got to lose? There's nothing to lose. What do you think? Huh? If you want I could introduce you to some ladies. Tomorrow? What do you think? Huh? FINCH? *[Pause.]* You know, the other day we were talking about you at the gym... *[FINCH stands slowly. THE BRIT stops talking. FINCH approaches him. They look at each other. Pause.]*

FINCH   Do you remember, Brit, that when we were kids you always defended me against the big guys? Remember, you were the one who taught me how to fight? And you always told me, "Don't let your guard down, FINCH, don't let your guard down." During all these years when I was about to give up I always heard your voice, telling me, "They'll walk all over you" Remember? Don't give up!... Don't give up!

[SKINNY and FATSO enter with the pizzas and the whiskey. THE BRIT has remained motionless with his glass in his hand. FINCH exits.]

SKINNY   Cough it up, boys. Five dollars apiece. And you fatso, as you bought a cake, it's five fifty six for you. *[He looks at THE BRIT.]* Hey, what's the matter? Don't you feel well? *[THE BRIT makes a gesture to say that he is okay.]* Do you know how hot it is outside? Everybody's in the street. Just like a bunch of cockroaches. Where did FINCH go? *[THE BRIT points to the exit. FATSO arranges the food.]* Hey, did I show you what my cousin brought me from Sweden?

FATSO   Did he bring you more magazines?

SKINNY   Magazines, my ass! *[He goes to a box and takes out an inflatable doll.]* Get a load of this!

FATSO   Hey, what a hot mama!

THE BRIT I had one... it only lasted two weeks.

FATSO   She left you for someone else.

THE BRIT She popped, you freak!

SKINNY   Hey, fatty, you're full of hot air, why don't you blow it up?

FATSO   What am I? The village idiot? *[Silence.]* Right! *[FATSO takes the doll and, resigned, begins to blow it up. As the doll begins to take shape THE BRIT and SKINNY start to talk, amazed.]*

THE BRIT Hey, she's better than my doll. Busty.

SKINNY   *[Proudly.]* Look! She's awesome!

THE BRIT Besides, she can't talk... what a great invention. *[The doll is now full size. FINCH enters. He stands there, looking at the scene. He has a harsh look on his face.]*

SKINNY   Fatso, tell the truth... how long has it been since you've had this kind of merchandise in your hands?

THE BRIT *[Hitting his own head.]* Hey, fatty! It's the answer to your prayers. I'm serious! It solves everything with the old ball and chain. Look! When she won't let you go out, all you have to do is blow up the doll. You put her in your bed, tell her you'll be there soon and then go about your business. Easy! No hurry. When you come back, she'll still be there! Waiting for you. Fresh as a daisy and ready for anything and everything. Huh, what do you think? Isn't it a great idea?

[FATSO looks at the doll and then begins to tenderly caress it. Pause. FINCH slowly approaches the group.]

FATSO   Hey, you know you're right. It's not a bad idea. *[Pause.]* Skinny, why don't you sell it to me?

SKINNY   Come on, Fatso! I just got it as a present. I haven't had a chance to try it out myself yet.

THE BRIT   *[Winking at FATSO.]* Go ahead fat-ass, seduce her. You don't have to ask permission. I'm surprised at you. *[Pause.]* Propose to her, and if she accepts...

FATSO   Don't start with me, Brit. I'm not in the mood.

THE BRIT   By me, you can do whatever you want. I thought it would be good for you. *[Taking FATSO to one side.]* If Skinny knows you're excited he's bound to give the doll to you.

FATSO   You think so?

THE BRIT   Of course.

[Pause. FATSO thinks for a moment and then goes to SKINNY.]

FATSO   *[Friendly.]* You're real lucky! What a babe! Just like a movie star! *[Talking to the doll.]* Allow me, ma'am. *[He offers his arm. SKINNY hands him the doll.]* I don't have much experience with this. Even less with a Swedish gal. But between the two of us don't you think we could arrange something?

SKINNY   Go slow, fatty. Not so fast.

THE BRIT   Easy fatty... A little class!

[FINCH, who has been to one side until now, moves behind the doll and begins to move its arms and head as if it were a puppet.]

FATSO   If you'd allow me, I would like to...

THE BRIT   *[Talking to the doll.]* He would like to...

[FINCH moves the doll's head in affirmation and extends her arms toward

FATSO.] She wants it, fatty! She wants it! We're off to a good start. *[FATSO and the doll, hug.]* Go on! Fondle her! Go ahead!

SKINNY Hey, pig, take it easy. If you pop her I'll kill you. *[THE BRIT sings the "Wedding March."]*

THE BRIT *[He ceremoniously gives the doll's hand to FATSO.]* Enjoy yourself, old man. You deserve it. Take good care of her. It's not easy in this day and age to find a chick like her. Isn't that right, Skinny?

SKINNY She's a real babe! A real gem!

[THE BRIT and SKINNY go to one side and pour themselves more whiskey. FATSO and the doll remain in the middle of the scene. FINCH is seated on the sofa watching the scene with a certain air of poking fun at the others. FATSO hugs the doll tightly and then caresses it. He kisses the doll. FATSO checks the reactions from THE BRIT and SKINNY.]

SKINNY Careful with your heart, fatty!

THE BRIT Don't stop now, you've almost got her!

SKINNY Let her have it! Let her have it!

THE BRIT Hey, fatso, aren't you gonna introduce us to your friend?

SKINNY Look, he's getting it on! You're driving me crazy. I won't last much longer.

[FATSO continues his exhibitionist game. SKINNY and THE BRIT begin to circle FATSO and the doll. They whistle, laugh, make comments, and pinch the doll. FATSO protects the doll as if she were a real woman.]

SKINNY *[In front of the doll.]* What a pair of... eyes. Yeah, baby!

THE BRIT *[Standing behind the doll.]* Look! Look at this ass! I'd like to lick you all over! You little whore! *[Imitating an animal.]* Grr.. .grr..! *[He bites the doll.]*

FINCH *[Interrupting the scene.]* Hey, guys, stop! *[To FATSO.]* Hey, fatso just carry on with it as if we weren't here. Get it? *[He winks at FATSO.]*

THE BRIT *[Reacting quickly.]* Of course! Excuse us! We didn't realize. We're a bunch of inconsiderate... She's all yours, man. All yours.

SKINNY You won her, fatso. Go on. Get on with it, that's all. Stick it to her. Look at his face. She can't wait any longer.

THE BRIT She's ready for it!

[FATSO is not sure what to do. The other three urge him on with gestures and words. They move FATSO toward the sofa, he lies down and FINCH places the doll on top of him. Pause.]

THE BRIT Hey, fatty, what are you waiting for? A blessing?

SKINNY Come on, fatty! Act like a man! Don't fail us now.

FINCH Can't quit now!

THE BRIT Come on, fatty! Come on, fatty!

THE THREE Come on, fatty! Come on, fatty!

[FATSO is not sure of what to do. Then he unzips his pants frantically. His face is red. The three begin to talk even more exaggeratedly. When FATSO embraces the doll, and wraps his legs around it, FINCH goes to the sofa and in one motion opens the valve on the back of the doll. The doll collapses on FATSO. THE BRIT and SKINNY look at FINCH.]

FATSO *[Shaking the doll as it collapses.]* What are you doing? Let me have it! Let me have it!

FINCH *[Unmoved.]* It's already after twelve. I'm going to hook up the DVD player and you, Brit, why don't you straighten up this mess?

[Long pause. The three are motionless. Slowly FATSO zips up his pants and removes the doll from on top of him. He sits up with the collapsed doll in one hand. He has his hand around the doll's neck. The body is completely lifeless in his hand. THE BRIT and SKINNY, without speaking, begin to slowly clean up the place. FATSO stands and walks back and forth with the doll in his hand. He looks like a robot, then lets the doll fall on to the couch. FINCH shows up with

the projector. He has made up his eyes and his mouth. He is dressed as a woman. No one seems to notice. He fools around with the remote, he whistles. A bell rings.]

SKINNY   It's the intercom. Let'em in, Brit.

[THE BRIT and SKINNY begin to accelerate their actions as they move back and forth straightening up the room. They look in the mirror and comb their hair. SKINNY checks his breath. THE BRIT sticks out his chest.]

SKINNY   *[To THE BRIT.]* You know Brit, the oldest is only eighteen. Imagine - only eighteen. *[Rubbing his hands together.]* What a night!

THE BRIT   I like'em young. They're still tender. *[They laugh.]*

SKINNY   *[To FINCH.]* Did you find the movies?

FINCH   Yeah. Which one should I show first?

THE BRIT   The one with the two girls... that'll set the tone.

[SKINNY has turned out most of the lights. One red light remains. He has put romantic music on the CD player. THE BRIT opens several bottles. FATSO remains seated with the inflatable doll in his hand. THE BRIT and SKINNY sit with a distinguished air about them.]

SKINNY   *[To all.]* I only ask you one favor... no noises. You already know... the neighbors... I don't want trouble.

[THE BRIT and FINCH agree. The doorbell rings. THE BRIT stands to open the door. He stops in the middle of the room and then returns to where the others are seated.]

THE BRIT   *[Lowering his voice.]* Hey, look, if I fall asleep, will somebody wake me up at seven...? Please! They're going to call me from the Cape at eight in the morning, and if I'm not home... I'm screwed! *[He has a scared look.]*

[SKINNY gives him a thumbs up. THE BRIT goes to the door. SKINNY looks over at FATSO who remains motionless. He nudges him so hard that the doll falls to the floor. FINCH turns on the television and it lights up on one wall of

the apartment. Blackout.]

AN ENTIRE LIFE

[THE FOUR are seated on a bench in the park in the same positions as in the first scene. They are between the ages of sixty-five and seventy. They are bundled up in winter clothes, with scarves, hats, and overcoats. They rarely move, but they look forward and occasionally look at each other.]

THE BRIT   Is it already eleven?

SKINNY   It's eleven.

THE BRIT   Eleven. It's still early. *[Pause.]*

FINCH   It's colder today than it was yesterday.

FATSO   It's less humid, that's what's going on. *[Pause.]* I don't think mother will make it through this winter.

SKINNY   You say the same thing every winter.

FATSO   Yes... but this is the last one. *[SKINNY coughs.]*

SKINNY   It'll be two years Monday.

FINCH   Poor Susie... she was so full of life.

SKINNY   You know, it's not good for a man to be alone.

THE BRIT   Well, you kind of get used to it... It's a whole lifetime. *[Pause.]* Little Lisa wants to get a divorce. Poor kids! I always say... why the devil do they bother to get married, huh? Why marry? *[Pause.]*

FINCH   This must be the coldest day of the year.

SKINNY   *[Looking out of the corner of his eye.]* You're always poorly bundled up. Are you wearing an undershirt?

FINCH   No.

SKINNY   So what do you expect? No undershirt! You're always the same.

THE BRIT   At noon I have to take my grandson to lunch. If I'm late my wife really gets on my case. *[Pause.]* When are you going to retire, fatty?

FATSO   Next year, God willing.

THE BRIT   You should come by the house some time and have dinner. Sylvia really likes you, she's always asking about you.

FATSO   I'd like to do that. But while mother's still in the same condition...

THE BRIT   You're right! You only have one mother.

SKINNY   Look at these kids, the way they fight.

FINCH   There's the little punk that shot at us with his water gun.

SKINNY   If I were his father, I'd give him one he wouldn't forget. There they go... the future delinquents!

FINCH   You know my nephew Charlie already became a lawyer. *[The other three act surprised.]* He graduated in two years. Two years! He's really a bright kid! He broke the mold!

SKINNY   Hey, you're more taken up with him than his own father.

THE BRIT   Well, intelligence is good for some things, but in this life you've got to be sharp, real sharp. If not, you're done for. Kaput! They run you right over. It's a good thing that Sylvia always made me keep my eyes open. *[Pause.]* I don't know what I'd have done without her.

SKINNY   *[To FINCH.]* How's your liver?

FINCH   *[Enthused.]* He's a real piece of work!

THE BRIT   Your liver? *[FINCH looks at him.]*

SKINNY   *[Pointing to his liver.]* Your liver? How's your liver?

FINCH   Oh, my liver... fine, fine. *[Pause.]* I take good care of myself. *[Pause.]* No fried foods. *[Pause.]* No fats. *[Pause.]* I don't eat at night. Partly because of my liver, and partly to save money.

SKINNY   *[Upset.]* Look, I've already told you a hundred times, but you don't want to listen to me! You can eat anything you want, but no salt! You don't need salt! It's poison!

FATSO   A lot of vegetables and a bicarbonate after every meal… that's mother's advice.

SKINNY   Your mother must be right, because she's nearly a hundred years old.

FATSO   *[Proudly.]* She's ninety-nine. She turns ninety-nine in December, God willing. You know she's a Capricorn, *[signaling SKINNY]* just like you, a really bull-headed.

SKINNY   Susie always told me I was a really bull-headed *[Pause.]* But I always respected her! She's the mother of my children.

FATSO   What? Is the hardening of your arteries cutting off blood supply to your brain?

SKINNY   I always respected her. *[Pause.]* Well, once in a while I'd get out of line, I'm only human! But it was always just little things, things that didn't matter much. I always kept the family out of it. Not like today, couples tell each other everything. Anything. Where will this all end? There's no respect. Everything is just sex and porn!

FINCH   I don't bother with meat. You waste a lot of time chewing. And then, there're always problems with digestion.

THE BRIT   Pasta is really good. I like pasta! With a little cheese and butter… no meat sauce.

FINCH   *[Disgusted.]* No meat sauce!

FATSO   Cheese dries up your intestines.

THE BRIT   Not me, not my intestines. But chocolate, yes.

SKINNY   *[Excited.]* What? Do you eat chocolate?

THE BRIT   Once in a while. Not all the time. When somebody offers it to me. Only once in a while…

SKINNY   That's bad! Very bad! It clogs up the arteries and you're a goner. My doctor always says, "Mr. Garret, you're doing just fine, but please don't eat any chocolate, not a single ounce, understand?" *[Everyone nods in agreement, impressed. Pause.]* Did you see where the Mets finally won? I told you so.

THE BRIT   They're all worthless, bunch of sellouts. Look, how could the Yankees lose at home! Come on!

SKINNY   You know now I can watch the games at ease. I don't have to fight Susie for the remote. Before, I could never watch a game all the way through! Not even dreaming! *[Pause.]* You know? I have insomnia. I can't sleep at night. *[Pause.]* Everything is so quiet! *[Pause.]*

FATSO   Mother's recipe for curing insomnia is to drink at least three quarts of water during the day. She says that the water flushes everything out, calms the nerves.

FINCH   You know, I get along fine with carbohydrates, what can I tell you?

THE BRIT   *[To FINCH.]* You should try the banana diet. It's the latest thing in the country. For breakfast, a glass of milk and two bananas. No sugar. For lunch, a glass of milk and two bananas. And for supper, a glass of milk and two bananas slowly baked in the oven.

SKINNY   I already tried the Atkins diet. I lost quite a bit. Look at these pants. See, how loose?... but after ten days I felt so weak I couldn't get out of bed. My daughter-in-law was so afraid that she called the paramedics... How embarrassing!

FINCH   Twelve hundred calories a day, that's plenty! Not an ounce more not an once less. *[Pause.]* Four ounces of vegetables. Three ounces of fruit. Two slices of bread. A glass of dehydrated milk. One egg, sweets, an ounce and a half. Butter, one ounce. Let's see, you add it all up and you get twelve hundred calories. Not a bit more or less. *[Everybody agrees amazed. Pause.]*

THE BRIT   My doctor, he's a specialist at one of those university hospitals, I don't remember where just now, but he's a really good doctor. He tells me to eat what I want without going overboard. That makes sense. *[Pause.]* But after that heart attack I don't feel like going overboard anyway. You know?

FATSO   That's why I touch my toes ten times every day. With the window open. I breath deeply and touch my toes. One right after the other.

FINCH   You have to take care of your heart. Don't push it too much. You never know, any minute it could go... and then, who are you going to complain to, the man upstairs? Forget it!

SKINNY   Right... there're lots of surprises. Without getting into it, look at all our friends who have already... *[Pause. THE BRIT stands.]*

THE BRIT   I'm going to go pick up my grandson. He's about ready to get out of school. If I'm late my wife will flip out. After all these years she's gotten to be an old grouch. *[He laughs.]* Well boys, we'll get together next Friday. *[They all agree.]*

FATSO   *[Standing.]* I'm taking off too. It's Mama's lunch time. It's like her stomach is an alarm clock! Well, boys, I'll see you all next Friday, God willing! *[The two exit. Pause.]*

SKINNY   That's right, there're so many surprises.

FINCH   Don't you think Brit's looking a little older?

SKINNY   You mean from last week?

FINCH   Yeah, more worn out.

SKINNY   You think so?

FINCH   Well, yeah! Didn't you notice? He looks henpecked. His wife is running him ragged. That's why... I'm telling you, it's better to be alone than with somebody and unhappy. What do you think?

SKINNY   What do you want me to say?

[THE BRIT and FATSO enter, but this time dressed as children the same as in

the first scene. They run onto the stage. They push each other. They make a lot of noise. SKINNY and FINCH look at them and, upset, move to the opposite side of the bench. We don't hear what the old men say but they are whispering with stern looks. The children begin to speak out loud, laugh, and shout, making a lot of noise. This invasion of privacy upsets FINCH. FINCH, frazzled, exits. SKINNY calls to FATSO.]

SKINNY   Hey, you there! Are you the one who shot at me with that water gun?

FATSO   No, sir! Not me! I don't even have a water gun, look. *[FINCH enters, dressed as a child. He signals to THE BRIT as if saying, "What does this old fart want?"]*

SKINNY   Tell your little friend, whoever he is, that if I see him again with that water gun, I'll make sure he remembers me for the rest of his life… Understand? You tell him that for me! Don't forget!

FATSO   Yes sir, I'll tell him. Don't worry. *[FATSO turns around, laughing. SKINNY moves away from him and says "Punks!" He slowly exits. The three children flip the bird and laugh.]*

THE BRIT   What an old fart! Why do they let them out of the old folk's home, huh? *[Laughter. He takes a deck of cards out of his pocket.]* Hey, look, look at these cards. I stole them from my old man.

FATSO   Hey, they're all naked.

FINCH   Does your old man play cards with these? I'd frame each and every one of them! *[SKINNY enters dressed as a child. A water gun is sticking out of his pocket.]*

ALL THREE Hey, Skinny, come over here! You can't miss this! Look at this! *[They begin to look through the cards, "Hey, what…" "Look at those…" Together they turn to the audience and begin to speak in unison, in a neutral tone.]*

Mystic Unio
Sala Babilonia, Buenos Aires (1991).

The deepest surface is the skin (Valery).

FIRE

WOMAN:
>-Why?

LOVER:
>-I am thirsty…

PROSTITUTE:
>-Are you coming in?

WOMAN:
>-He
>stood before me
>displaying the evidence
>in silence
>in silence
>holding himself in my gaze.
>At that instant
>all life froze.
>The air
>My God!
>The air

dry ice.
My body
a trembling hole
and all he said was
"It is true, my blood
is contaminated."

PROSTITUTE:
-I did not know I was possessed
by the plague...
How was I to know?
This plague
is a cursed chain.
Nobody knows where it begins
and I almost don't want to know
where it ends.

LOVER:
-Poor
poor love.
Always living with such fear.
Each inch of your skin
bearing so much fear
and now you have finally found
in this sickness
a cause
that justifies that feeling.

WOMAN:
    - And he simply said
    "My blood is contaminated"
    Of all hells
    this hell.

    Why him?
    Why us?
    Why anyone?
    And of all the "anyones"
    Why him?
    Why us?
    Why?

LOVER:
    Why?
    Now we really are nailed
    to this game
    of precise limits
    pre / cise.
    Time.
    Space.
    How much longer?
    How long?
    What sort of drama must be unfolding
    inside of me
    where everything is invisible.
    Who now is

now is

the protagonist

and playing the role of a lifetime?

WOMAN:

-Questions

questions

that do not calm the hell.

They only twist the mind

into tongues of fire.

If there is a God

I ask:

Why me?

Why him?

Because of his weakness?

Perversity?

Treachery?

Betrayal?

No!

It is too great a punishment.

I

his wife

would forgive him a thousand and one times

if necessary.

And I know it is necessary

because inside of me

-in this long history

of humiliations
and lies-
I have killed him
a thousand and one times.

PROSTITUTE:

- I don't want to think

WOMAN:

-She doesn't want to think

PROSTITUTE:

- I give my body over
to lethargy.
Thinking about what happens
It is always painful.

WOMAN:

-She doesn't want to think
it is painful.

PROSTITUTE:

-Better to let it happen
and be distracted.

WOMAN:

-She doesn't want to think
it is painful

better to be

distracted.

LOVER:

-No, not distracted!

From the first time

I knew

with all my senses

I knew

that this would be a tragic encounter.

Passion

as the only language

is always tragic.

Invariably

it ends up devouring

itself

in its own fire.

PROSTITUTE:

-Bonfires.

Tragedies.

Words.

No need to complicate things

so much.

This is my work

and this is what I know how to do

I do not even need to find them.

They come to me like as they might a doctor.

Looking for the equilibrium.
they have lost.
Of course they are not satisfied
or enthusiastic.
Of course not!
Why would they be?

Need
is always slavery.

LOVER:

-Mysterious energy
you draw the sexes together
until they become one,
I know that I took advantage of you
without managing to decipher
your most profound intention.

WOMAN:

- We won't give in
my love
my man
mine
as we never
give in to anything
not even to ourselves.
But I need to trust
believe
that this fight belongs to us

only
exclusively
to the two of us.

PROSTITUTE:
-It is always the two of us.

LOVER:
- The two of us.
Between the two of us
in the two of us
there were certain moments
when the bodies
were not enough
to perform such a dance
and then
all that remained was to look at one another.
And it was there
that I discovered
that the Fire was turning
into Light
inside of me.

PROSTITUTE:
-We are always two
two bodies
only two bodies
honest

transparent
like bodies are
when they cannot deceive
or be deceived
I am fortunate
to deal in them.

WOMAN:
-How could you deceive me
when I couldn't?
My betrayal
remained trapped in my mind.
Impenetrable seed
that lets
nothing
in or out
for fear
-always fear-
that it might become rooted
and grow into a tree.

I was and I am
stone.
To be able to contain
the seed
of desire.

LOVER:

    -Then
    Light is the first step
    but, what
    is the last?
    I feel a tremendous thirst
    not for closeness
    but for true communion.

PROSTITUTE:

    -The bodies
    come together and move apart
    to the rhythm of the heart.
    It is the music
    of water and fire
    and of the whole universe.
    My ears do not know
    a better melody.

LOVER:

    -What will become of you?
    What will become of me?
    Always with fear.
    Always making the wrong move.
    Inopportunely.
    Swinging at the void.
    Asking permission.
    Howling in silence.

In silence.

You made me know of
thirst.
I am thankful to you
but
what will become of you
who have paused
just beyond your skin?

WOMAN:
    -Why him?
    Why us?
    What will we have to pay?

LOVER:
    -What will we have to learn?

PROSTITUTE:
    -In life
    everything must be paid for
    I have certainly learned that lesson.

HEAT

LOVER:
    - I am thirsty…

PROSTITUTE:
    - Are you coming in?

WOMAN:
    -Why?

LOVER:
    -Mysterious energy
    you who draws the sexes together
    to dissolve them into moans
    I confess
    -confronted with death
    and its truths-
    that what I know of you
    is almost
    what animals know
    and it is
    almost
    what everyone around me knows.

WOMAN:
    -Prostitutes.
    Lovers.
    Semen wasted
    and now cursed.

Why should I sacrifice myself
mortality
for one
who has not selected me
for pleasure?

PROSTITUTE:

-I never choose
I allow myself to be swept by the tide
without intention
without impulse
I do not have preferences
I only stay afloat
available
and lagging behind.

LOVER:

-I will not cry
I am not going to cry
I am not going to cry
no
I won't.

Life
-how ironic-
life
returns our own actions to us.
That is the great justice

and the great understanding.

I wonder
-now
that we are defenseless-
this trembling
what will it bring back to us?
What image
in what mirror?

WOMAN:

-I don't...
know...
how...
to react...

Abiding with him is a monster
that cuts my head off
while it warms
my feet.

And I no longer know
who I am
or what
brought us together
once.

LOVER:
>   -In this long night
>   of threats
>   I sense that you will also confess.
>   Tell me:
>   You penetrated many bodies
>   but have you ever
>   have you ever
>   grazed a soul?

WOMAN:
>   -A soul?
>   I hate you with all my being
>   You hurt me at my most vulnerable place.
>   My pride.
>
>   I hate you
>   You needed
>   a wife
>   lovers
>   prostitutes
>   and a never ending lair
>   to hide your frailty

PROSTITUTE:
>   -It is useless.
>   I don't remember him.
>   I don't know who he is.

One man's tracks
are erased by the next.

WOMAN:
-I hate you
above all things
because your blood and my blood
can no longer
mix to create
but exactly the opposite
yes
listen closely
"exactly the opposite."
And that is why
I need you to explain:
What stirred your blood?

LOVER:
-What stirred you?
Was it excess?
Simulation?
Artifice?

I begin to understand
that life's fluids
-how ironic-
do not admit
vulgarity.

PROSTITUTE:

    - Vulgarity?
    If I am like an animal
    that gets used to everything
    and repeats its rituals
    without modifications
    day after day.

    I don't want to know.
    I don't like changes.
    That is why I am always moving
    spinning
    spinning
    above myself.

WOMAN:

    -On the edge of the abyss
    the only thing that comforts me
    is:
    That you are you
    and I am me
    and down there
    or up there
    lies
    the net
    of all that has been established.

PROSTITUTE:
>   -Undoubtedly
>   as sickness invented the doctor
>   sick love
>   such as –you are you
>   and I am me–
>   undoubtedly
>   sick love
>   invented me

LOVER:
>   -I desire you
>   in that discovery of Light
>   In that sensation
>   of no longer existing.
>   Of standing
>   erect over the horizon
>   of time.

WOMAN:
>   -I desire you
>   in that time that you told me.
>   In your eyes
>   lies all the truth
>   Look at yourself
>   and learn.

PROSTITUTE:
>- I don't desire anything
> everything comes around.

LOVER:
> -Fragile
> fragile
> pulling
> love
> I have meditated
> and faced with the inevitable
> unprotected as I am
> mind and guts
> suspended
> in a mortal future
> I want to offer this passion
> and all its energy
> so that
> the heat might consume your pain
> and transform it into a cure.
>
> It is my most powerful wish
> and I offer it
> gratefully.

WOMAN:
> -No
> thank you

If I was not your wife
at that moment
now
that I am trapped
inside the ritual of abstinence
now
in this abstinence
I do not want to be your mother

LOVER:

-I wish
aspire
that this heat might
consume your pain
and make it into a cure.

PROSTITUTE:

-Don't I know who he is?

WOMAN:

-Don't I know who I am?

LOVER:

-Don't I know what it he is?

PROSTITUTE:

-I will not cry.

I will not cry.

No.

I am pregnant

with horror.

I know

 I can tell by the looks

of disgust

and scorn

of all those who fill the churches.

LOVER:

- It is a moment of alchemy.

If coal turns into diamond

that scorches my entrails why can't this wild fire

be turned into

heat,

warmth,

glow?

WOMAN:

-I wish

aspire to

find a place

to rest

and dream

that all this

is nothing more than a dream.

PROSTITUTE:

>-From their infected souls
> they curse my body
> and my blood
> but even so
> I will not change.
>
> If necessary
> I will change landscapes
> and gazes.

LOVER:

> -By the Grace of love
> The less I name myself
> the faster
> the fire
> turns into ocean.

PROSTITUTE:

> -If the only thing that I know how to do is
> open myself and spin
> around my self
> like a flower
> like a flower
> like a fetid flower.

LOVER:

> -By the Grace of love

The less I remember myself
the faster
the fire
turns into ocean.

WOMAN:
-They avoid me
Run away from me
Why must I bear your cross
if our the pleasure
was so scarce?

PROSTITUTE:
-Don't I know who is he?

LOVER:
-Don't I know what he is?

WOMAN:
-Don't I know who I am?

I am no longer your wife
or your mother
or your daughter
or your sister
Who am I?
Only a witness
to the unnamable?

Is that all I am?

LOVER:

-I avoid myself
I run away from myself

WOMAN:

-My love…

LOVER:

-To continue
intact
I need to trust
In the thirst of miracles
and not
in the tears of tragedies.

WOMAN:

-My love
I swear
that in those moments
I would like to be braver but
from where will I extract
that which does not exist?
You taught me doubt
in all its forms
and fear of the truth
Now
you see

> I doubt
> even my own eyes.

LOVER:
> -Love,
> you look like a child in your helplessness
> and my breasts
> overflow with compassion.
>
> Compassion for you
> and for all of us
> who got
> beyond your skin.

PROSTITUTE:
> -I don't expect anything
> everything comes around.

WOMAN:
> -I am marked
> through my veins
> circulates desire
> and impotence.

PROSTITUTE:
> -I am marked
> And I am only a link in the chain
> An empty vessel

that receives wounds.

LOVER:
- I am marked
I have witnessed the lightning bolt
of the eternal
and I know
that it is only the first step.

LIGHT

PROSTITUTE:
-Are you coming in?

WOMAN:
-Why?

LOVER:
-I am thirsty…

WOMAN:
-He
stood before me
with proof in hand
in silence
in silence
holding himself in my gaze
In that instant
all life froze.
The air

My God!
The air
dry ice
My body
a trembling hole
and all he said was…

LOVER:

- A miracle?

PROSTITUTE:

- A mistake?

WOMAN:

-A bad dream?

Or maybe this is precisely
a dream
but one about the most intense desires?

PROSTITUTE:

-A mistake?
For the first time
I would like to remember
I wish tracks
did not fade so quickly.

LOVER:

    -Each of us
    Such infinite spaces!

WOMAN:

    -Are you healed?

    And now you want
    to begin again
    With what?
    If there are no traces
    of innocence left
    in our hearts.

LOVER:

    -Are you cured?

    Now you want
    to continue
    With what?
    passion became Light
    and the price of vigil
    is detachment.

PROSTITUTE:

    - Are you healed?

    And now you want

        to end it
        With what?
        If I never started anything
        I have only been
        a recipient
        of disgust.

WOMAN:

        -A dream?

LOVER:

        -A miracle?

PROSTITUTE:

        -A mistake?

WOMAN:

        -Now you say that you are complete
        but inside I am hurt.
        Don't act as though
        I could build on
        quick sand.

LOVER:

        - Beloved
        if you could only understand
        the look in my eyes
        while gazing above.

If you could only understand
the murmur of my deepest desire.

Then
maybe
you could understand
this miracle.

PROSTITUTE:

-A mistake?
Maybe.

Maybe
senses
are only the vehicle
I am also questioning
in secret.

LOVER:

-Then
you should know
that your death and resurrection
were the springboard
sending me into
what I still don't know.

WOMAN:

-I try to ignore you

annul you
absorb myself.

but the louder
I scream out my existence
the stronger
you burst into my throat.

PROSTITUTE:

-Maybe
senses
are just the vehicle
because now I know
that without searching
I have searched
in each body for
the sublime.

LOVER:

-My beloved
you would also understand
that in this new loneliness
I am going to find myself
where I need to find myself.
There
where there is no consistency
where there is barely being.

WOMAN:

    -You burst in!
    You burst in!
    You burst in!

PROSTITUTE:

    -You burst in
    and with memory
    doubts arise about intensities
    of pain and pleasure.

LOVER:

    -I am not abandoning you
    I am just going to find myself.

WOMAN:

    -Sorry love
    I too was and am
    afraid.

    Nobody taught me
    the secrets of life.

    No one ever discussed with me
    about the secrets of death.

    But I was raised and taught

only about

the unnecessary.

PROSTITUTE:

-Instead

with me

everyone experienced "the little death"

for an instant.

I have grown so accustomed to its visit

that I have converted

each gesture

each act

each of my words

into

a testament.

LOVER:

-Each of us

such infinite spaces!

WOMAN:

-Yes

I was only raised and taught

about

the unnecessary

and now I learn

even from the wounds

of pride.

I learn that
the deeper the roots
the better the fruit.

PROSTITUTE:

-This corrupt pregnancy
Is funny
It has in the end
given birth to a desire
where I imagine a future
At last a desire to imagine a future!

There are some mistakes
That are enough.

LOVER:

-I am thirsty
not for closeness
but for true communion.

WOMAN:

-I have been an eternal beggar
I always went for profits
plundering affections and pleasures
conditioning every exchange
demanding voraciously

and here I am
empty
empty
But now nothing can be the same.

Now I need to perceive love
as the only reward.
Only then.

LOVER:

-Within the eternity of the present
In the silence
I trust
and surrender.

I have known
passion
and compassion.

Now nothing can be the same
I ascend one more step
and the thirst
is intense.

PROSTITUTE:

-Like a stone rolling around
at the bottom of the lake
a terminal look

Sirens' Song

Fundación Banco Patricios, Buenos Aires (1995).

Knowledge may only be accessed through the threshold of the body (Valery).

Song 1:   Desire
Song 2:   Loneliness
Song 3:   Meaning
Song 4:   Passion

Song 1: *Desire*

SHE:

I am a beautiful animal, I practiced my movements for thousands of years
until they've become round, subtle.
I trained the air I breathe until able to express
what always ends up inexpressible.
What can't be pronounced. Only exists.

I am a fascinating animal who, with each chosen fruit, lifts herself higher.
Even when my genitals are weighed down, nailed to the ground.
Even when my sex screams out and my mind bursts into thousands of splinters.

I am a successful animal. I lie with ease.
I seldom say what I think.
I'm seldom clear on what I feel.

But in those moments of stillness and silence, in those moments, yes,
my pain is sharp, my entrails do not deceive me
and lucidity is a scorpion's sting, poisoning me with what I desire
and fear at the same time.

I am an animal who wishes to be god.
And who lives asking herself, blinded by panic and justifications.
How many things must be left behind without looking back?
How much lifeless energy is needed to swim upstream?

I have reached the perfection of my animal nature.
My instincts have always cradled me.
I have taken pleasure through each of my orifices.
until I'd had my fill
and, its repetition has already become unbearable.
Stupid.
To the point of wanting… to lift the lid off my brains
with just a howl,
a precise, precise sounding knife
releasing the pressure.

Yes, circling the tracks has its advantages.
But today, none of that is enough.
I am possessed by rebellion's desire
I want to partake of all the forbidden fruits.
Fleeing from those numbing Edens that only multiply divisions.
Good. Evil.
But I learned, as my bones waste away and my fur thins,

that each thing contains its opposite.

Necessarily.

That there are no loose gears.

Everything is connected through wounds and sutures.

From my rational animal nature,

my spine petrified from trying to keep my sights on the horizon of dreams,

I wish to choose every instant

of my life and my death.

I rebel against anything alien.

Against anything moral. Law or command.

I have heard everything I needed to hear, and obeyed all the orders

like the good pet I am.

Centuries frolicking in limbo.

Feeding. Drinking. Copulating. Birthing.

Licking my scabs.

Bearing the heavy weight of my breath after ingesting decayed meats.

I have said everything I had to say. Rarely the truth.

I have always followed directions.

 Cross. Do not cross. Now, yes. Go ahead. Stop.

The comfort of allowing myself to be swept by the tide.

Each morning I begin a repetition of tics. Of tacit conventions.

Like the rising sun and the moon.

I file my nails. I polish my teeth. I perfume my cadaverous breath

to leave for the depths of the jungle,

a paradise of zombies, frightened by the number of awards and punishments accumulating day after day.

I believe I choose and only obey electronic voices.

I believe I am free and worse than a circus dog, proud of its bonnets and bows.

I desire and I am afraid. Desire. Afraid.
Loneliness...
-I've never known the depths of that frozen secret.

I rebel against the need that expels me to the outside of myself
on all fours, drooling, flesh exposed,
through the black desert of pain.
I rebel against time and space.
Against blasphemies and blessings.
I rebel against the whole animal kingdom,
to claim another throne.

The horns are filed.
The skull has been molded over a low flame.
I am ready to receive the crown.

Song 2: *Loneliness*
SHE:

Which wounds, which sutures, which marks on the body
must be produced to, at last, be able
to cancel the decline of tissues and cells?

How do you pass through *the everyday*?

To break the habits?.
At first... the simplicity.
I feed on herbs alone.
I abandon all comfort. All ornament.
I distance myself from my passions... even from my slightest distractions.
If I choose to fly, any interference, no matter how fascinating,
ends up being an anchor.
I set my own alarm clocks.
I walk on tiptoe.
I communicate only through signals.
I keep one eye shut.
Each movement commands
an encounter with my willingness.
For long hours, I let my eyelids fall
and focus my attention on my mind's black hole.
The skull's machine shoots off, crazed.
And it projects a scene I had chosen to forget a while ago.
"Birds of prey circle above my open body."

A sharp pain in my stomach. A knot in my throat.
I press harder still on the crown.
The known, the familiar, erupts like a siren's song.
I move back more and more.

In the blue night,
I hear the moan of my beast in heat.
It yearns passion. Scratches the earth. Slaps its buttocks.
Desperately needing friction with another body, to shoot sparks.

But no one, nothing is around.
Only the beast and its trainer.

The beast understands no needs other than those of its skin.
It screams and spits towards the four cardinal points.
The trainer hopes the animal will tire.
That it forgets itself.

Cross. Don't cross. Now yes. Go ahead. Stop. Stop. Stop.
The comfort of allowing myself to be carried by the tide.
Now yes. Go ahead. Now no. Stop. Not now. Stop. Stop.

Lucidity is a scorpion's sting.

Now, that the contours are disappearing
and the stimuli's intensity fades.
I see how my life slips away through the wounds of memory,
and I do not know if I am dreaming
or if what happened before was a dream.
I do not know if I am caterpillar or butterfly.
I don't know if I am the night, the dream or the dreamer.

I do not want to disappear
without having peered through the eye of the one who sees everything.
No, I do not want to disappear…

Song 3: *Meaning*
SHE:
Here are the scars from so many mutations.
Deep wrinkles on my face for opting to take the risk
of that which still is nameless.

So many alarms were necessary.
Stones in my way and in my shoes.
Each step, a decision.

And now I am only a spot.
An empty dot, filling the void.
Without time. Without place.
The perfection of completion.
Nothing. No one.
A desire wandering in space.
Unalterable.
Forever.
Forever?

Is that the price?
Forever.

How I would like to be in peace.
To feel that it is the end of a long journey.
That the desert stars blinded my longing
and I no longer expect anything.

But that's not it.
No, that's not true.
Lucidity is a scorpion's sting
Poisoning the blood of dreams.

Completeness smells of death,
of something useless.
My solitude frightens the birds of prey.
These hands have stopped scratching the ground
and now they are roots
that grow inward
and don't give seeds.

I know, I can perceive reality clearly, with my eyes closed.
I can control the wasting away of my cells.
Stop breathing for long periods of time
And confront the threshold of death.
A dream within a dream
that I always wanted to experience
with open eyes.

I know it, and it's not enough.
None of it stops the howling.
The restlessness.
The pinch of doubt.
I am a dot. Closed off in its emptiness.
Drop of water. In the blue desert.
My voice is inaudible.

There is no one to hear it.
My eyes see nothing more than unchanging horizons.
There are no bodies that cross my eyelids.
And I no longer understand why I am here.

Nothing. No one.

I don't leave tracks.
I am going to disappear embracing the sand,
which in turn, will disappear under my weight.
Static.
And I don't feel peace. Or gratitude.
Solitary flights turn out to be sterile.

Lucidity...
more and more, I feel this heavy cross
of carrying myself on my shoulders, for so long.
While there, in the jungle, life erupts.
Like always.
Like fireworks.
Like laughter and tears.
Like... the celebration of those who bow humbly
before the mystery.

Something is giving away.

Song 4: *Passion*
SHE:

Something fails.
Something is missing.
I decide…do I? To return to the jungle,
to its endless wandering.
Something fails.
Something pulls me.
I widen my vision
and density is uncovered in its chaotic exuberance.
Here we are again.

I observe...
The frailness of the coverings.
The constant fear of being expelled, after tasting some fruit
of pleasure or knowledge.
I observe limits and repetitions.
Tremors. Cries. Nightmares.
Each thorn embedded in the stomach's pit.
The need that expels us,
on all fours, drooling, naked,
beyond the black desert of pain.
Grief. Grief.
Yes, something's failing.

I discover, in me, something that beats

Something that doubts.
Something that says, where there is pain, is a sacred place.
Lost in thought, I observe.
An animal licking its wounds in silence.
An animal that licks the wounds of another animal,
 in silence.

Life, fever,
breaking through the cracks of my memory.

I feel how my chest, involuntarily, yes, involuntarily,
Expands, shattering to pieces the crown on my skull.
My spine can take no more.
Desire pounds its scorpion's sting.
Time begins to flow through my veins.
 My skin retracts and I grow old.
Once again, my heart beats unsteadily.
Now yes. Stop. Now yes. Stop. Now yes...
My throat gasps and sighs.
So much vulnerability astounds.
Nothing is foreign to me.
Nothing.
I am yet another beat within the great beat.
I am each eye, each fingernail, each serpent bite.
Need.
Wound.

Solitary flights are always sterile.

They never fly beyond the illusion of power.
I rebel against all kingdoms.

I am an animal licking its wounds in silence.
An animal that licks the wounds of another animal,
in silence.

Paradises Lost

Sala Morocco at the Primer Festival Internacional de Teatro [First International Theatre Festival] in Buenos Aires (1997).

An unknown place, obstinately desired, as if it had ever belonged to us

-I stopped loving you when I unveiled all your mysteries.

-You are by my side and you speak of love and I watch you and I know not who you are.
What are you doing here, talking to me about love? What rules, what games, what ceremonies did we perform to get to this place?
And now everything is set up in such a way that I truly do not know how to ask you ... who are you? ...what are you doing here?... what love are you talking to me about?

-Your needs and my needs coupled in a perfect coitus.
You adjusted to my mounds, filled my holes.
And then, without realizing it, we obliged ourselves to go on committing.

-I await you against all hope.
For me, true tragedy is a life incapable of exuberant gestures.
Like that butterfly, that, so afraid of having her wings cut, goes through life passing as a caterpillar.

-Those were intense, passionate times.
And today they remain echoes, fog.
A cramp in the pit of the stomach.

-All is possible in the name of love
I love you if you love me, but if you leave me I want you to disappear from my life, from life itself.

I love you so much and I want that much in turn. No more, no less. However, if the balance is in my favor, all the better. I will save up for rough times.
I love you and I want to become the only one for you, necessary, indispensable.
But please, I ask you, do not smother me.
I love your generosity, your kindness, your solidarity.
And above all, I love and demand that it all be exclusively for me.

-I believe I love you because I like sleeping with you on cold winter nights.
But I don't know, because when spring comes, I also like waking up alone, not knowing exactly what to expect.
I believe I love you because when I am afraid, your body, your hands, calm me down and give me the peace of the newborn.
But I don't know, because when I feel strong, sometimes your hands weigh me down and bury me in boredom.
I believe I love you because in the silence I lose myself in your gaze and nothing exists outside of you.
But I don't know, because sometimes I long for a cataclysm so you'll disappear from my sight once and for all.
I believe I love you because when we make love, it is so intense that I could kill you, split you in two.

But I don't know, now with no desire, the very idea that everything repeats itself makes me desperate.

-What made me betray you?

-I left you and now I look for you.
I look for you knowing that one day I will leave you.
I shall leave you before you leave me.
Let me look for you, but please do not leave me.
I don't want anyone to look for me because I don't want anyone to leave me.
Thank you for not letting me look for you and for not looking for me.

-Thank you for this monotony.

-Who are you? You tell me that you have been with me for a while. We sleep, we eat, we bathe together... but who are you? How did you get here? What tunnel did you slide through?
Or was it me, distracted once again who opened the gates for you?
You look at me as if I were yours, as if the game were in place and definitive.
And I swear that I do not know who you are.

-What made you betray me with in oblivion?

-I have always claimed that I loved solitude, but I am always willing to open my doors and make room in my bed.
Actually, I really cannot bear can't stand not having someone to tell how I love and need solitude.

-I need you so I won't find my emptiness.

I love you to feel loved.
I am jealous of you so that you will take care of me.
I care for you so that you will choose me.
I complement you to create needs in you.
What do you expect? This is how I learned.

- What is the ideal distance between solitude and suffocation?
Where to stand between fear and asphyxia?
Between the I and the we?

-Your commitment dampened desire, passion.
You became a part of me, and then
I needed to look for something beyond myself
that completed me and set me apart.
That's how the trio began.
As did the tragedy.

-Some love others for being an inextricable part of themselves
Others love because we are completed in the union.
Choices become impossible.
Even to imagine.
The tragic situation grows.

-I want you wild only to be able to tame you.
I want you strong, just so the pleasure of breaking you
can be even more intense.

-The desired body is never the conquered body.

No better or worse.
Never the same.
-I am addicted to provoking adoration, fascination, intensities, commitment.
And that's why I suffer from chronic suffocation.

-When the tongue moves faster than the heart
everything crumbles.

- When I am longing, I wonder where in my body the longing is installed.
And when I wonder about missing, I stop missing.
The sensation disappears in the eternal, complete, and unique present instant.

- Not fleeing. That is the key.
Confront the mirrors.
The silence. The stillness. The mind's ghosts and enticements.
The corrosive acid of self-pity.
Not to run away. That is the key.
Remaining in the void.

-So many times my fantasies have become reality
that now I am afraid to fantasize.

-There is some grandeur in solitude.
It is a straight line to our origins.

-At a certain age, we must commit to a daily battle
with our muscles, with our flexibility.

So that the body doesn't begin to close itself off like a vindictive oyster.

-I am a locomotive transporting dozens of frightened little girls.
Some see only the locomotive.
Others, only the little girls.
All are mistaken.

-Why do I desire one body and not another?
Perhaps because of fixations, primary sensations which formed the appetites?
Desire for familiarity or its opposite?

-Why does a certain body unleash my desire for unity, for fulfillment, for fusion?
Perhaps fascination, mystery?
Weakness, the possibility of total possession?
The annihilation of the other, and thus, of desire?

-All movement is a search.
All encounter, a difficulty.
All need, slavery.

-I have dreamt of you so much
that a parallel history has been constructed,
where I am only an impotent witness
unable to manipulate beginnings or endings.
I witness, innocent, the language of souls.
And upon awakening, in the materiality of vigilance,
I only find the silence and perplexity of what I have sensed.

-I would like to share only a few things with you
Such as:
Traveling the world.
Enjoying creation in all its manifestations.
Laughing and crying.
Exhausting words and silences.

-Who am I going to blame? Which part of myself?
Because not all my parts want the same thing.

-Guilt permits us to traverse skins, but not to settle.
Guilt permits pleasure, but not plenitude.

-This state of relaxing, in silence, in stillness,
without pain in the body or the soul.
 Without cold or heat. No hunger, no thirst.
This neutral state, latent, almost imperceptible
surely must be what they call happiness.

-Nothing is better than monotony to make one believe in peace.

-What will become of me without your shores,
me who was the sea and adored you?

-I am afraid of change.
I am afraid of being responsible for the profits and losses
of all change.

-The life of love sails in a sea of memories and fantasies,
of ghost and mirrors.
And when the tide goes in, all we find on the coast is photographs, letters, poems, discolored unrecognizable objects.

- Upon reaching such peaks of intensity, what remains?
Repetition or death.
It is all the same.

-I want to annihilate you before you annihilate me.
Your gaze splits me in half.
Your hands, astute, compromise my surface.
And they take away all that is left of my will.
I retreat, but I am addicted.
I approach you, and you consume me in your addiction.

-I hear my animal cry.
There is no tongue that could heal this wound.

-Do you care for me? Do you care a lot? Do you love me? How much? To what lengths? Am I yours? Are you mine? Do you love me? As much as I do? Are you my love? Are you my life? Are you telling me the truth?
Should I believe you? You aren't deceiving me? You won't leave me? Do you love me? How can I be sure? Do you care for me?
Forever? Really?
And so it goes, long hours, long nights and days.
Entire lives.

-Go away, you are smothering me.
But please, don't go so far that I cannot find you
when I need to feel smothered.

-I am running away. I am searching for fresh air. Something new.
And then I fall into other eyes. Another mouth. Another voice. Other questions.
Other fears.
And all that is familiar is repeated without variation, once more.
But the mere idea of a new escape weighs on me.
So I conclude that I have found the love of my life.

-Is there anything less loving than self-love?

-You are a mirror where finding myself scares me.
Because your passion for me throws me off.
Your love for me makes me vulnerable,
Your surrender ties my hands.
Your need paralyses me.
Your longing debilitates me.
Your desire pushes me away from myself.
And I want to tell you that I am no longer willing to wear old costumes.

-In love, we should flee from perfect moments.

-How is it that an institution such as the family
is based on something as unstable as feelings?

-Living together is a monster that decapitates while warming feet.

-I like our parties and our laughter.

I like your foundation that supports internal earthquakes without collapsing.

I like your eyes, mysterious slits where the starts reveal themselves.

And your gaze so ancient, so old.

-It is hard to be an odd number.

Asymmetry threatens even numbers.

They are afraid of losing their balance.

-True loneliness belongs to the one who is different.

Psychological loneliness.

-I want to abandon you in the sweetest moment.

So that an abyss opens up under your ribs.

So that, for your body, memories of me are like a whirlwind, quicksand. A sudden blaze of whispers.

-I fed up with saying words that later I cannot recognize.

-To miss someone is like crawling after images,

like a slug under the sun.

- How does one prevent dreams from coming true?

And then turning into daily life, routine?

How does one prevent dreams from turning into nightmares?

-I cannot resist the attraction for the abysmal.

For the constant stitch in the pit of the stomach.

-When will the day come when passion is only heat, radiance?
Memory of fires.

-Passion and possession are eternal playmates.
Impossible to know one if the other is not present.

-I try to melt into another body, letting my orifices be filled.
And I take possession of theirs, of their protuberances with fury and desperation.
I catch my breath and the feeling of failure.
I remain singular.
One mystery can never melt into another mystery.

-If we were not made to possess and be possessed,
why do we have arms, fingers, legs, feet, tongues, teeth, penises, vaginas, anuses, nipples?
We would be flat, impenetrable.
Moons of flesh, moons of blood.

-I imagine your voice bursting forth in the night
announcing to me that everything is possible
within the territories of desire.

-I have already cried for you. I have asked for your forgiveness so many times. I already repented. I changed already. I learned. I told you so often that I love you, that I finally freed myself of you.

-We use others to tell our stories.
And we do it as many times as necessary, until we can understand them.

-I only want you because, with your insolence, you opened the door to all desires, by opening me and opening yourself.

-If at key moments, I could imagine how people with common sense act and then allow myself to do just the opposite, I would save a lot of time.

-In love, it is not he who loves the most who suffers, but he who loves himself least.

-The wall crumbled down, and your eyes looked through mine like two swords of fire and tremor.

- I remained thirsty for you. Hungry for you.
Is that what they call nostalgia?
Younger sister of sadness?
Daughter of desperation?

- I can be with you and give myself over without reservations, because I know that I will never fall in love with you.
To fall in love is to lose oneself in the other.
And at this stage, I want to find myself.

-Is there anything worse than to live remembering that time when you were happy?

-I idealize you because I need to believe that I once lived a love story in capital letters.

-In triads, be careful of edges.
Those there either hit bottom or rebel.
- What propels life?
Because I can't stand this repetition of daily rituals,
fulfilling duties, running errands, acquiring new toys,
pretending to be distracted,
dreaming of miracles… while growing old.

-They love me in a way that is going to annihilate me.

- They love me in a way that every choice rips me apart.

-In desperation, the meaning of life disappears and energy along with it.
That is why we cry, because nothing else can be done.

-If I did not forget that I am here to learn to give,
that everything else is anecdotal,
I would save so many lives.

-I go from symbiosis to biting,
from symbiosis to bite
and so on.

-In many love relationships, if I take away the narcissistic game,
there is almost nothing left.
Almost nothing that has to do with the word love.

-My excessive movements are horrific.

-Everything goes by. Delicacies are quickly evacuated.

-Those times when I was profoundly cross-eyed, I confused freedom with leaps into the void.

-To love is to stimulate and to boost up the other's power,
even if it enables him to do without us.
The trap lies in the fact that it is hard to do without someone who loves so wisely.

-One has to live with friends and share very special moments with lovers.
But we always do the opposite.

-I was fascinated by our differences.
Everything I could not understand about you.
I worked. I made a tremendous effort to mitigate them. To fit you into my mould.
Today I leave you, victim of a ferocious boredom.

-And I ask him, and I ask him, what's going on?, and he tells me and I tell him, that it is not what is going on, and he asks me, how do you know?, and I tell him what is going on, and what he has to say, and he tells me, oh really!, don't tell me?, and I tell him, and I tell him to tell me the details, the particulars, and he tells me he has nothing left to tell me, and I don't believe what he says, and I tell him, come on, tell me what you have to tell me, because if not, I am going to tell you, and he tells me, ok, tell me, and I tell him, and I tell him.

-An orgasm is like letting oneself be caught up in a whirlwind, and passing out.
Like dancing until exhaustion.
Like feeling a spilt at the pit of the stomach.

Like standing on the edge of the abyss and wanting to fly.
It is the explosion of the inevitable.
It is losing the limits between bodies and be a single heartbeat.
It is spilling voluptuously over another skin, like boiling lava.
It is watching a solar eclipse and go blind.
It is abandoning the last refuge, to be bareness.

-I am in the midst of a retreat.
Not only will I not cross great waters
I won't even take risks with bidets.

-Nothing here, nothing there.
and suddenly, out of the top hat of consciousness,
jumps the yellow rabbit of madness.

-What can be said is not enough.
Everything is betrayed by time.

Zero

Along with *Hormigas en el bidet* [Ants in the Bidet], *Zero's* original version was directed by Ricado Holcer and performed in Espacio Cendas (1999). The play was a part of *Combinatoria de 8 en base 4* [Combination of 8 in base of 4], a show featuring the works of several dramatists.

The fish dies by the mouth.
The fish says that he does not want to lie.
And when he says so, he lies.
The fish bites the bait.
Kisses the hook. Wants to taste it.
It's his nature.
The fish dies by the mouth.

1.

In semidarkness, we see two bodies, close to each other and motionless.

    HE   an embrace
    SHE   one of those embraces
    HE   silent
    SHE   one cheek against the other
             the scent of perfume
             hair still wet
    HE   the earlobe between the lips
    SHE   the tongue inside the ear
             slowly

>
> slowly
>
> testing
>
> very slowly

HE   it runs over the neck

SHE   the nape

HE   the curve of the neck

SHE   the hand on the nape slides softly

> upwards
>
> over and over again

HE   another hand, brings the head to the chest

SHE   agitated

HE   toward the softness and heat of that surface

SHE   ever more agitated

HE   the hand presses the head

> while the mouth slides towards the womb

SHE   the waist arches

HE   while it slides down

SHE   the nails mark the back

> the bottom

HE   a tattoo

SHE   sweat on the forehead

> in the cracks

HE   at the beginning of the pubis

SHE   make-up smudges on the sheets

HE   instructions in the ear

SHE   ……

HE   the mouth open, wide open,

> bites the shoulder

SHE	without a moan
HE	the teeth don't stop pressing
	until the skin tears
SHE	blood leaves tracks on white
	next to make-up
HE	only much later is the prey released
SHE	more instructions
HE	…
SHE	asks for the mouth to slide over there
HE	the legs open
	the body's full weight on its heels
SHE	the unbearable urge
HE	he holds back as long as he can
SHE	she asks
HE	he holds back
SHE	she gives up
	loses herself
HE	one mouth approaches the other mouth
	the fish kisses the hook
SHE	the lips
	throb
HE	they part

Lights dim.

2.

The lights come up, we see a woman in her forties. She is at a small area of the stage. While most of the space remains in semi-darkness, at another section of the stage, we see a man's silhouette.

SHE:

I always arrive early.

I don't mind waiting.

Quite the contrary.

I need to get acquainted with the turf.

Avoid the unexpected.

If I am going to bare my body,

-and of course I am not just talking about taking my clothes off-

I need to trust my surroundings.

That's why I arrive early.

I want to get ready very, very slowly.

As if I were doing it late at night,

in an unknown hotel, in front of an open window.

Settling into this new air

is like placing the dress on the chair.

Delicately.

Without haste.

One cannot always enjoy waiting.

Waiting that doesn't make the palms sweat or the heart race.

The calm of not exposing signs of weakness.

Not a single crevice in which fear might nest.

Yes, I choose this way.
Once again.
And I wait, stripped of expectations.
But of course, it wasn't always like this.
Not too long ago,
there were other times
of deep sadness.
It was hard for me to realize that certain embraces
held more hate than love.
To discover that passion's ups and downs,
concealed a tremendous violence.
Pleasure before submission.
That love's murmurs could quickly turn to insults.
Into blows. Tears.
Into the panting of a beast. In heat.
Many nights, too many nights
necessity obliged me to remain alert.
Time suspended, as interminable as desire.
The conquest, always devastating.
Did it have to reach this point?
Was it necessary?
I did not know then.

For years I pretended it didn't matter.
The unbearable didn't matter
It didn't matter that I was torn to apart.
Not seeing didn't matter.

Not listening. Not saying.

It didn't matter that air went through me like an old rag.

But I got that far.

Then I couldn't keep on surrendering.

Who can?

Who can forget herself that much?

Not me.

Now I know.

My vagina would retreat in the face of fear.

Anguish would end up building a space between my skin and another's.

During the night, in the silence, captured in the breath of that other body,

so loved, so hated,

so loved,

voices would emerge.

An obsessive choir. Maddening.

"Are there already signs of decay?

Should I be getting bracing myself for the final break-up?

Or perhaps I should take the lead, and annihilate him first.

It's either him or me. Yes, him or me."

And even if the sheets were still warm and damp,

in the face of such a monologue,

a thread of tension

would run through my body, from head to toes.

And it would settle in there.

In the pit of my stomach.

Poor puppet.

Poor, poor, puppet, gasping between spasms and sighs.

But here, in this neutral place,
nothing prevents my mind from going blank.
Zero
I am a perfect zero.

Here, contact is just that.
A nervous touch.
A trained ear that tries all combinations
until it manages to open what was
a few minutes ago,
sealed.
And I abandon myself because I am not afraid.
And I am not afraid, because I don't feel any need.
Not even the slightest desire that the encounter
with the one who is now waiting behind the door
would last any longer than necessary.

In this rented space there is only convenience.
A well-drawn contract.
Intimacy within limits.
Nothing to protect or preserve.
No one to thank.
To betray.

And if the service is lacking
I can change,
and change and try and change again,
without getting upset.

I have all the freedom to do so.
Nothing is tying me down, nothing at all.
Only the determination that each time be different.
A painstakingly planned adventure.

An adventure where I discover that nothing,
nothing at all compares
with the pleasure of directing our own scenes.
And little by little, almost without realizing it,
becoming accustomed to the sweetness of power.

Here I pay a fair price, at my whim,
with my unbridled imagination,
to let myself be carried
far away
by his agitated breath on the nape of my neck.
To feel his body, competent, pressing against mine
until it makes me burst.
Until it makes me feel like a puddle. A thing.
Without will.
Something available. Ready to respond.
To anything.
To anyone.

I don't know if he,
the man who in a few seconds is going to enter into my desire,
whom I already know and who knows me,
perhaps better than anyone else.

Will be available next time.
And that makes each time
the last time.
Each encounter forces me to go further still,
toward the unknown in me.

The light is artificial.
The arrangements, my smile, my voice,
are as artificial as the light.
To a certain degree a place to rest.

Two knocks are heard.

Not yet!... I will tell you when...
(*To herself.*) Not yet...

Lights dim.

3.

Lights come up on other section of the stage. We see a man in his late twenties. The lighting in the area where the woman was standing remains in semi-darkness; yet, her silhouette may be perceived, sometimes immobile, sometimes in movement.

HE:
I am the man waiting behind the door.
I have orders to stay here.

To wait for her signal.
I observe the closed door.
It reminds me of other closed doors.
And now, I don't even try to predict the scene
on the other side.
They are always the same.
The woman changes, but what happens inside,
the preparations,
are part of a routine.
Stupid.
They wash. Put on make-up. Try different postures. Movements.
Gestures.
They check their breath by blowing on their open hand
close to their mouth.
They examine themselves in the mirror.
Obsess over their shape,
as if appearance mattered in this case.
And it doesn't.
Not at all.
When they finally call me
and I enter through the door,
I stop being who I am.
Immediately.
I empty myself.
I come to desire what the woman desires.
The one on the other side. Waiting for me.
Damp hands. Racing heart.
And before her, I become a recipient.

A perfect thing that satisfies her longing.

All my movements are aimed to her consuming gaze.
Her quality control.
I change my accent.
The way I pronounce words.
I become a foreigner.
Someone who is not ready to dialogue.
To engage in conversation.
And in this way, our heads
-contaminated by frugality,
by monosyllables and longer and longer silences-
become indolent.
A sheer crawling after something like
instinct.

I don't expect a thing.
She seems to expect everything.

The last time, with this same woman,
something unpredictable happened.
Unpredictable: a strange word to be used
by someone who says he does not expect anything.
But yes, I recognize that there was a subtle variation
in the painstakingly planned script.
By her. Of course.
She, the one who pays.

When we said goodbye,
I could not help noticing her mouth, was half-opened
and trembling,
as if she was about to say something,
something that for some reason
she did not dare say.
After a few moments of hesitation, she closed it.
Her mouth. She closed it.
Firmly.
And left, almost running.

What could she want?
More of the same?

Meanwhile, I, the one here behind the door
still waiting,
I would like, how I would like!
for everything to be over by now.
For no one to be on the other side.
Waiting for me.
Monitoring my performance.
Pondering if her money was well spent.
If today was better than last week.
If it will be different next time.
If not, better to change
as soon as possible,
because the novelty has already worn off.

There are moments when I need to sink my fingers in the sheets

for fear that my hands will aim for her neck.

And squeeze.

The worst thing is, that I know that she wouldn't do anything to stop me.

That she would take pleasure until the end.

The same way she does with everything.

No, she would do nothing to keep me from subduing her.

The thing is sometimes my hands are not satisfied.

They don't give in.

They don't understand anything about profits. About contracts.

They hope for another skin and this one appears.

So submissive. So ready to be touched.

When the only one they miss is the other skin.

The one that retracts.

The rough one.

The one that is hardly ever available.

At that very instant when I am about to embrace her

I want nothing more than to open the other door,

the forbidden one.

Open it. Enter the darkness of the night

where he waits.

Not for me.

Or not just for me.

Search for him in the shadows.

Place myself with his men.

Be one of many.

Doubled over with jealousy,
wait my turn.
Let myself be driven like a novice
by his skillful hands
into the depth of my own flesh.
Beg him for more, more, and more.
Until I explode.
And even then, more.

While she takes pleasure under my body,
Begs for and takes pleasure.
When she gives me everything
everything that one body can give another
and allows me in wherever I want
in any possible way
and accepts that I won't kiss her mouth,
won't kiss her
ever
on the mouth,
and allows everything
because for her there is no other way
than to pay
and wait
and try
and pay
and wait.
I watch her, there under my body, and in her face I see myself.
I am she

waiting my turn
in line
behind the other men
all horny
all furiously desiring
to be chosen
to go through the doorway
to finally
find shelter from the elements.

I am she
in her insatiable need
in her fragility
in her half-opened mouth and her eyes blank
in the way she waits
and ravages herself.

One of these nights
my fingers are going to let go of the sheets
and she is going to ask for what she always asks for,
and I am going to tell her what he tells me
not to breathe anymore,
to breathe
not to breathe anymore,
to breathe
not to breathe anymore
as a last gesture.

Lights dim in this section of the stage.

4.

The lights illuminate the whole stage. The two characters are standing still in here, their own respective areas. While they say speak the following text...

SHE   I am yours.
         I like to say, I am yours
HE   I am the bait.
SHE   I like to be able to say it. I am yours.
HE   I am just the bait.
SHE   I don't love you.
         I will never love you.
HE   Suspended from the hook
SHE   I want to close my eyes. Make them blank.
         Blind.
HE   I am the bait that disguises the hook.
         That provokes hunger.
         Flesh covering the flesh-cutting blade
SHE   I am yours.

Lights gradually dim until the stage backs out.

She

Teatro Payró, Buenos Aires (2005).

We see two men wrapped in towels from the waist down. The rest of their bodies, naked. Onstage there are some wooden benches. IRIONDO is seated. MARLEY is partially reclined. Even their slightest movements are very slow. Their bodies are covered in sweat. A dense vapor impregnates the atmosphere. At times characters exhibit their nakedness freely as is typical in a masculine space.

1.

IRIONDO	I hate this!
MARLEY	It is supposed to be enjoyable.
IRIONDO	Taking care of your looks is never enjoyable.
[Pause.]	
MARLEY	Why are you here?
IRIONDO	….
MARLEY	A request?
IRIONDO	What?
MARLEY	Yes, did someone asked you to pay more attention to your looks?
IRIONDO	No…
MARLEY	No, of course not…
IRIONDO	Why do you say that?… *"No, of course not…"*
MARLEY	No reason.
IRIONDO	I don't believe you… Tell me… I'm interested.
MARLEY	Nonsense, I was just wondering… *[Sitting down.]* Is She…young?

IRIONDO   Ah, that's so that's it.

MARLEY   Youth is demanding.

IRIONDO   And contagious.

MARLEY   Do you think so?

IRIONDO   Don't you know about that?

MARLEY   Why should I know?

IRIONDO   I don't know, I thought…

MARLEY   What?

IRIONDO   It doesn't matter.

MARLEY   No, now it's my turn, tell me…

IRIONDO   *[Watching him carefully.]* I thought… that with such a careful appearance… Why would a man take so much care of himself if not to conquer? And a man of your age… what is it he wants to conquer?

MARLEY   You're wrong. You speak as if we were all…

IRIONDO   Forgive me. There are exceptions, of course. *[Pause.]* Look, you're right. I'm not here just for me. No, this is more like a sacrifice. A torture *[Laughing.]* The last resorts of a drowning man. *[Serious.]* But, no, this isn't about seduction.

MARLEY   I've never seen you before.

IRIONDO   I've never come here before. *[Pause.]* A man trying to win back a woman makes a fool of himself. Look at me, I've tried to lose weight, keep my hair from falling out, do 200 push-ups a day… I even thought about dying my hair. *[Pause.]* And deep inside, I know, I know for sure that all this is useless. If that desire exists, it's elsewhere. That's what's expected in another story. But I don't know what. Sometimes there's no place to rest… everything seems… to be made of paper.

2.

[IRIONDO and MARLEY are seated on the same bench.]

IRIONDO   She went on a trip… a vacation, with her husband.

MARLEY   Honestly, I'm not interested.

IRIONDO   For a month. To the sea.

MARLEY   That's not so long…

IRIONDO   No. I miss her, I can't sleep.

MARLEY   There are pills. I take a couple before going to bed.

IRIONDO   In the midst of my insomnia, I have fits of crying, of anger.

MARLEY   Excuse me, but I don't think so much intimacy is… appropriate.

IRIONDO   I break things. The first thing I find, I smash against the wall. Alarm clocks, telephones, lamps. It makes me feel better. It gives me relief.

MARLEY   You should see someone.

IRIONDO   Who?

MARLEY   Someone that can help you.

IRIONDO   I come to places like this so that I can sleep a little later on. It's the only way.

MARLEY   It's getting late… *[He gets up to leave.]* Until next time.

IRIONDO   You know who I'm talking about.

MARLEY   *[Stops.]* Me?

IRIONDO   Yes, I've seen you two together several times

MARLEY   Sorry, but… you saw me with who, several times?

IRIONDO   Her red hair is like fire. It's hard not to notice her. And her height… now that I see you standing, She might be taller than you. I guess that's why She stopped wearing high heels. Just to be considerate.

[Pause.]

MARLEY   Are you… her husband?

IRIONDO   No. Her lover. Just like you. Another.

[Pause.] [MARLEY begins to laugh. Little by little. Fitfully. His laughter is bitter. IRIONDO ends up laughing, too. Then, gradually, they fall to silence...]

3.

[They have the same expressions as in the previous scene. However, they have switched places.]

MARLEY   Have you followed me?

IRIONDO   Just... for a few months

MARLEY   Why?

IRIONDO   Why?!... It's obvious...

MARLEY   I mean... why *now*?

[Pause.]

[They stare at each other, sizing each other up.]

IRIONDO   I found a poem... in her purse. I am not saying that it's right to snoop, but sometimes it's necessary.

MARLEY   And?

IRIONDO   Her husband can barely sign his name. I have to admit that the poem was quite good. Cheesy, but with some original touches: *"Trapped in your net... let me be swept up by the tide of our embrace... etc, etc, etc."* It's yours, right? Or you never know... It was signed "Your insatiable... explorer..." or something...

MARLEY   ....

IRIONDO   I burned it. It burned like toilet paper.

[MARLEY, with a violent expression, advances a few steps toward IRIONDO, who backs off.]

MARLEY   What do you want?

IRIONDO   To know. To know a little more. I also feel cheated.

MARLEY   How long...?

IRIONDO   What does it matter?

MARLEY   Of course, it matters! How long?!

IRIONDO   For quite a while...

[MARLEY and IRIONDO are a few feet apart. Facing each other. MARLEY'S arms are at his sides. Fists clenched. His breathing is agitated. He looks like he is about to jump on IRIONDO, who is on guard.]

4.

[Each of them is standing on opposite sides of the room. They are as far apart as the space will allow.]

MARLEY   I also suspected something.

IRIONDO   Tell me... As I told you.

MARLEY   No. I don't think so...

IRIONDO   We might laugh even more.

MARLEY   I doubt it...

IRIONDO   Listen, we'll probably never even see each other again...This is a unique opportunity to get to know our beloved one a little better.

MARLEY   I don't trust you.

IRIONDO   I don't trust you either, of course. But this is not about trust. We are checking the facts. That's all.

MARLEY: ....

IRIONDO: You have one version, I have another. Don't you want to know how *Frankenstein* was created?

MARLEY: Don't call her that.

IRIONDO: Why not? Passion is always somewhat monstrous.

[Pause.]

[You can tell that MARLEY is struggling to decide whether or not to speak.]

MARLEY   One afternoon... *[IRIONDO sits down.]* She seemed to be in a great hurry, very nervous. She told me that her husband was waiting for her in his studio... that he had seemed strange lately... and we'd have to take some time off. When she left, there was something in her kiss... in the look on her face before entering the elevator, something that made me close the door and go directly to the phone. I called the studio, asked for him. I was told that he was out of town, and wouldn't be back all week.

IRIONDO   Let me remember... September of last year?

MARLEY   It's possible...

IRIONDO   Yes, I gave her an ultimatum.

MARLEY   You?

IRIONDO   Why are you so surprised? I knew about her husband's trip, and I could not understand why we were seeing each other so little. Until then, I wasn't suspicious. I hadn't realized that lying was already a part of her very breath. *[Pause.]* What were you going to do if he answered the phone?

MARLEY   Hang up, I suppose. But I knew he had nothing to do with it. Her anxiety and excitement... didn't fit with a long relationship. Do you know what I mean?

IRIONDO   Perfectly. Habit brings out a lot in someone... but never excitement. And... did you stay calm? Didn't you try to find out more?

MARLEY   No...

IRIONDO   No?

MARLEY   My wife... *[He interrupts himself.]*

IRIONDO   Don't worry, I know her too. Remember that I followed you. And one thing leads to another.

MARLEY   Bastard!

IRIONDO   Your wife must think the same, about you. When I saw her she was pregnant. Did she deliver? A Girl? ...A boy?*[MARLEY is trying to restrain his anger. His face is red with fury.]* I don't have children. We always thought that it would happen someday... but no. Something wasn't right. Maybe it was for the best.... *[He smiles bitterly.]*

MARLEY   Are you married?

IRIONDO   Of course, what did you think?

MARLEY   I don't know. *[Pause.]* I have three kids.

IRIONDO   Congratulations.

MARLEY   My wife is... someone very special. I love her. I love her dearly.

IRIONDO   Again, congratulations. But let's be honest, here, in this place, we are not talking about "love." We are talking about something else. Passion. Hunger. Thirst. Right?*[Pause.]* I also feel something very special for my wife... so special that sometimes, I don't know what it is.

5.

[IRIONDO is seated with his back to MARLEY. MARLEY is standing observing him.]

MARLEY   It's very annoying; it's enraging to know you're being watched.

IRIONDO   I wasn't following you. Why should I care about your life? I was watching her. I needed to know how far She would go.

MARLEY   And?... How far?

IRIONDO   You see? You also want to spy on her. But, without getting your hands dirty, of course. No, I won't tell you. Enough is enough. *[He stands to go.]*

MARLY   Wait... wait...

IRIONDO   I won't tell you! Go do your own dirty work!

MARLEY   *[Blocking his way.]* On Sundays... when She tells you she's going to the country... do you see her? Do you meet? *[IRIONDO starts to laugh.]*

MARLEY   Answer me!

IRIONDO *[Holding in his laughter.]* Yes, sometimes. But *my day*, my day is Wednesday.

MARLEY The day She goes out to dinner with her friends.

IRIONDO That's right. And believe me, it's true about dinner. Sabere. Sabore. Which day is yours?

[Pause. MARLEY hesitates. IRIONDO insists by staring at him.]

MARLEY Monday.

IRIONDO Ah... acting classes? *[MARLEY nods.]* And we all know, all about those late night party people. Bohemians. Yes, I remember when She asked me if she was too old to take acting lessons. The art of lying with truth. I said, no, quite the contrary. Age adds experience. And with experience, one lies better. More sincerely. But I never imagined....*[Pause. They stare at each other.]* I want to smash your face in.

MARLEY And I want to run you over with my car... put it in reverse and do it over and over.

IRIONDO Every moment you become more and more... disgusting to me.

MARLEY We agree... once more.

IRIONDO I try to imagine... what you could have awakened in her? What kind of interest?

MARLEY And I look at you... and it is frankly pathetic! Sad!

IRIONDO Careful!

MARLEY What bothers me the most, is admitting that I don't know her as well as I thought I did. Why... what need?

IRIONDO Yes... what need?

MARLEY Your presence here... is clear proof that I have no idea...

IRIONDO About what?... her vices?

MARLEY Stop it.

IRIONDO What amazes me, about her is... She always goes for more.

Without limits, but the contrary... She's lured by excess... doubling her bets... Such an extraordinary lover! Do we agree?

MARLEY   That's enough. Shut up!

IRIONDO   What's the matter? Perhaps you think perversion is exclusively yours? Or maybe that deceit exists, but only for everybody else? Or... that danger is a proof of love? Something like, "*I am taking risks... I am yours.*" No! No! No! No! You're completely wrong! You're hallucinating!... You poor fool!

[MARLEY jumps on him. They wrestle. Fall to the ground. The lights dim. The stage is in semi-darkness. The silhouettes of the two fighting bodies are perceived. This lasts almost a minute. Then silence.]

6.

[The men are sitting in their original positions. IRIONDO has a cut close to his mouth. And MARLEY has a wounded neck and his left eye is black. There is a long uncomfortable pause.]

IRIONDO   Where did you copy it from?... the poem.

MARLEY   It's mine. Don't be stupid.

IRIONDO   I've read it somewhere. You probably took it from the editorial pages? of some newspaper. *[Pause.]* Do you know what I do for a living? I'm an editor.

MARLEY   And...?

[MARLEY stands up with effort. His body is very sore.]

IRIONDO   Are you leaving? I wanted to propose something to you.

MARLEY   Let me guess...You want me to leave her. And move aside to let you three be happy?

IRIONDO   Your mind is painfully lineal. No, I wanted to propose... that we kill him.

MARLEY   Who? Her husband?

IRIONDO   Yes.
MARLEY   …
IRIONDO   And then, we share her.
MARLEY   …
IRIONDO   She'll be under our control. She'll be able to meet our needs at our convenience.
MARLEY   You're totally insane!
IRIONDO   It must be a lack of sleep. But it's a good idea.
MARLEY   Impossible, I can't stand you, I could never…
IRIONDO   I know, I know, this pact would never be possible between friends. It has to be like this. Between butchers.
MARLEY   You speak about killing… as if it were like pressing a key and deleting.
IRIONDO   Do you suffer?… Do you suffer for her?
MARLEY   What do you care?
IRIONDO   Do you think it is reasonable to suffer for love?
MARLEY   Nothing seems reasonable when it comes to love…But what are we talking about?! I've had Enough. *[He walks towards the door.]*
IRIONDO   We don't use protection… when we have sex. I was wondering if you…
MARLEY   *[He stops.]* What?
IRIONDO   *[He changes his tone.]* "Don't put it on… I want you so much…" Yes, it seems She says the same thing to everyone.
MARLEY   Everyone!… What do you mean?
IRIONDO   That we don't know… that we don't know anything. For example, right now, do we really know where She is? Can you swear that She's with her husband? She could also be with her husband and a new lover. I can't imagine her

life… without that adrenaline. *[MARLEY is in a state of shock.]* *[Pause.]* Did She get in touch with you?

MARLEY   …

IRIONDO   Did She call you?

MARLEY   …

IRIONDO   She calls me every morning and tells me how bored she is…And I don't believe her at all. She tries too hard to show her boredom. You understand, right?

MARLEY   Every morning?

IRIONDO   It is an old habit, wherever She might be.

MARLEY   How long has it…?

IRIONDO   Years, years… years of pain.

MARLEY   Then, why are you so determined to keep at it?

IRIONDO   Who's determined, idiot?!… It is inevitable! It is an addiction! It's something you can't control. My body only responds to her desire. Do you know what that's like?

MARLEY   *[Hesitant.]* Yes…

IRIONDO   Do you know what that is like?! No, no, I don't believe you. That need… that animal urge that makes me forgive her everything. Everything! Even the fact that She got involved with an idiot like you! *[He comes closer to the back wall and hits his forehead against it several times.]*

MARLEY   Calm down…She told me…

IRIONDO   *[Mocking him.]* She told me, She told me, She told me… Please!! *[He continues banging his head against the wall.]*

7.

[IRIONDO is seated. One hand holding the towel to his forehead. He has a pained expression.]

IRIONDO   What did She tell you? She… what did She say?

MARLEY   …

IRIONDO   Let's see, let me guess…Her eyes shining with love, her voice cracking… She whispered: *"You… are my only love."*

MARLEY   Stop it!

IRIONDO   How's it my fault?… if She always says the same thing.

MARLEY   But, what do you want me to believe? That She never stops…?

IRIONDO   *[Interrupting him.]* I wouldn't say that She is a pure nymphomaniac, but… the description comes close.

MARLEY   Stop mocking me! I know her…*[Corrects himself.]* a little… She can't pretend so convincingly.

IRIONDO   She fakes it so well that she convinces. I mean… just listen to yourself: *"No, that can't be true, I know her. Well, a little."* *[Pause.]* On Mondays… doesn't She go to acting class? She's obviously a fast learner. She has talent and very good teachers.

[Pause.]

MARLEY   And … why does She take risks, why doesn't She use protection with you, with me, or let's suppose with… *"all the rest of them?"*

IRIONDO   Good question… we'll have to ask her. As for me, I am not particularly interested in going on living. And you?… A married man, a man sowing his seeds… who, out of pure laziness and vanity, chooses to believe… a whore.

[MARLEY comes closer to IRIONDO. He stands up. MARLEY puts his hand on IRIONDO'S chest and pushes him several times. IRIONDO lets him and doesn't react.]

MARLEY   Don't call her that! Don't you ever call her that again! In just a few minutes you have managed to throw everything into the gutter!

IRIONDO   You're right. I'm sorry, my nerves are shot. I'm suffering from abstinence.
Sometimes, There are moments when I'd like to throw myself against the wall. Damn her! I hate her! I loathe detest her! *[He flops back onto his seat and bends forward. His hands holding his head. His head rests in his hands]* I want her so much! I want her so... so... so much!

8.

[MARLEY walks around, restlessly. IRIONDO remains seated with his eyes closed.]

MARLEY   She...

IRIONDO   What?

[Pause.]

MARLEY   No, nothing.

[Pause.]

IRIONDO   What?... I'm waiting... What?!!

MARLEY   Your relationship...is it...passionate? *[They stare at each other for a few moments.]*

IRIONDO   Fire!... I melt in her arms and she in mine. When we are done loving each other –physically, I mean–it's inevitable, I smother her with kisses, her face, every inch of her body, over and over again, and during those times, I'd like to build an altar to her...
There's so much joy!

[Pause.]

MARLEY   How, how can it be?...

IRIONDO   What?... Is it the same for you?

MARLEY   After each orgasm... She clings to my body desperately. Eyes full of tears. She begs me never to leave her. And I feel her body trembling with passion. Surrounding to my desire. During those moments I know I could do anything to her... kill her... split her in half.

And the embrace, the embrace is so intense, that it seems then that only one of us is breathing. Sometimes She asks for things...

IRIONDO   Stop! Stop it now! I can't bear it! *[MARLEY reacts as if he is coming out of a trance.]*

IRIONDO   Why don't you leave? Go! Go! Enough! We already know too much, don't you think?

MARLEY   Yes, yes ... you're right...

[Both remain still.]

9.

[Both have the same expression and position as in the previous scene.]

MARLEY   And her husband?

IRIONDO   I forbade her to speak of him. It turns me off totally.

MARLEY   She told me a few things.

IRIONDO   She has to pour it out to someone.

MARLEY   A typical story.

IRIONDO   Did I ask for details?

MARLEY   I thought you were still interested in creating...

IRIONDO   You still can't say *Frankenstein? [Pause. They size each other up. They exchange challenging looks.]* Alright, go on! Now, here with you, it's not a problem for me to cool off, on the contrary. Besides, from the glimmer in your eye, I can tell that you enjoy the idea of telling me certain things. Things that, most likely, I will not like at all. At all...But, be careful, don't step over the line. I can heat up again at the blink of an eye. And I'm less and less aware of my own limits.

MARLEY   With a preface like that, I don't feel like talking anymore.

IRIONDO   But, what do you expect, you animal?! You think this is an everyday conversation? Two guys in a bar, having a drink, talking about pussies. *[He approaches him until he is almost touching him. They are nose to nose.]* I bleed! Do you get it? I have a wound... and I bleed! *[Pause.] [IRIONDO walks away. He assumes a listening attitude.]*

MARLEY   It's actually quite a common story.

IRIONDO   You already said that, *"a typical story."* What else?

MARLEY   He abandoned her, neglected her for a long time... trying to work his way up the corporate ladder.

IRIONDO   *[He starts to laugh.]* "Trying to work his way up..." poor guy!

MARLEY   When he finally made it, there was already a distance between them...

IRIONDO   Insurmountable.

MARLEY   Yes...

IRIONDO   Distances must be insurmountable to exist. *[Pause.]* What does She tell you? Why doesn't She leave him?

MARLEY   He threatens her. He has told her that, if She leaves him, he'll kill her. Or himself. He has told her many times. He can't stand the idea of living without her.

IRIONDO   That makes two of us. *[Pause.] [IRIONDO looks at MARLEY as if demanding a response.]* And...?

MARLEY   And what?

IRIONDO   Could you take it?

MARLEY   I... I have my children. It's different.

IRIONDO   Of course, family comes first. *[Changes abruptly.]* Hypocritical snake! I could swear that we're three, and four, and five... a massacre! And everything... because of flesh... and its urges, so infantile. *[Pause.]* What... what makes her so powerful? Have you thought about that?

MARLEY   No...

IRIONDO   No? You don't think. You don't feel. You don't act. A happy man!

MARLEY   Actually...

IRIONDO   Yes?... What?

MARLEY   ......

IRIONDO   Come on, go ahead!... spill your guts... just like I am here with you. Can't you see that I'm serving them on a plate?... offering them to you? Eat!... Eat!...

[Pause.]

MARLEY   Several times after an encounter...

IRIONDO   Yes?...

MARLEY   After we part, I sigh, relieved, that it might be the last time I see her. That... frivolousness, that carefree feeling lasts for hours, sometimes even a few days...

IRIONDO   Yes, I know what you're talking about.

MARLEY   And then, I don't know how, what triggers it, but her presence begins to invade my mind, slowly... gradually.

IRIONDO   It invades everything.

MARLEY   Her image, the memory of some precise moments, become almost an obsession.

IRIONDO   The same movie plays here *[He touches his head]*

MARLEY   The rest disappears. Fades away. I struggle to stop it from happening.

But it's useless... I no longer exist for the rest, I'm no longer around.

IRIONDO   The wait begins...

MARLEY   My mind on hold... I only wait for the signal. Like a lap dog.

IRIONDO   Trained to satisfy the monster's voracity. Nothing satisfies it. It needs a pack of lap dogs.

MARLEY   Shut up!... Don't go on!... I am sick of you! Your comments disgust me! And I assure you... that I'm not planning to leave you an out. Besides...

IRIONDO   Yes?

MARLEY   Never mind.

IRIONDO   No? *[Pause.]* You never thought about running away?... Leaving everything behind?... Starting a new life somewhere?

MARLEY   ......

IRIONDO   We discussed that many times. And I was the one who resisted. The idea of the daily routine horrified me. I was scared the routine would end up annihilating the desire. And without desire?... No more altars, no more offerings. The desert. No escape.

Now I regret so much precaution, but it's too late.

MARLEY   She doesn't want to?

IRIONDO   It's too late...

MARLEY   Maybe... because now she's talking to me about it.

IRIONDO   *[With a closed fist, he swings at MARLEY, who barely manages to duck.]*

Do you want me to rearrange your face?

MARLEY   *[On guard.]* Yes, I do! And what?...You imbecile!... Morbid jerk! Asshole! *[They throw several punches at each other, which both manage to avoid, until IRIONDO hits MARLEY in the middle of his face. MARLEY is in pain, he touches his nose and sits down. IRIONDO follows him and stands before him.]*

IRIONDO   So, what you just said is true?
MARLEY   *[Hurt.]* No...
IRIONDO   It's better that way. *[Pause.]* So... have you considered my idea?

10.

[MARLEY'S towel is stained with blood. He is lying down on one of the benches. IRIONDO paces around anxiously.]

IRIONDO   It's simple. Either we kill him, or he kills her. Sooner or later, he is going to find her out as I did. He could also kill her, and whichever lover happens to be with her that day. I don't deny that the possibility makes the idea more appealing.

MARLEY   Why do you suddenly believe her? Maybe She's just exaggerating and her husband is only trying to keep her at any cost.

IRIONDO   Most repeated threats are carried out. I've read about that.*[Pause.]*Never mind, I knew I couldn't count on you.*[Pause.]* *[IRIONDO starts to cry inconsolably.]*

MARLEY   What now?
IRIONDO   ......
MARLEY   Look at yourself... you're pathetic!
IRIONDO   ......
MARLEY   Come on!.... Stop it!
IRIONDO   *[Between sobs.]* Mutilated... I feel mutilated.
MARLEY   Don't you think that's a bit too much?
IRIONDO   No!... Unless holding her in your arms is the same to you as holding a magazine. And judging from that stupid expression on your face, that must be true. My God!... but why, why you?! Why did She choose you? You are completely worthless!

MARLEY Not that again! *"Nobody loves her like I do… nobody suffers like I do."* You make me sick! *[IRIONDO has stopped crying.]*

[Pause.]

IRIONDO Do you think that fidelity is possible?

MARLEY It's a possibility.

IRIONDO Do you think She would feel faithful to each of us?

MARLEY …..

IRIONDO She's happy. She doesn't seem to feel any guilt or remorse. It's strange, don't you think? Since I met her, I've wanted to get inside her head, and see how it works… Now I'd like to know how She can go from one body to another… o lightheartedly, so easily.

MARLEY *[He comes closer, they stand facing each other.]* Did he hire you to follow me?

IRIONDO Who?

MARLEY Her husband.

IRIONDO You're an idiot! Look at me, do I look like a hired guy? *[Pause.]* And what about *her*? … do you desire her? I'm not talking about her… not her… but the mother of your children.

MARLEY Leave my wife out of this! She has nothing to do with this. She's not a part of this scene.

IRIONDO Mediocre petit bourgeois! *[He mimics him mockingly.]* *"Don't mess with my wife. She, poor cuckold, has nothing to do with this."[MARLEY comes closer looking threatening. IRIONDO backs off.]*Listen, I couldn't care less about your wife and the kind of relationship you two have. Besides, you don't have to be a genius to guess…What I'm trying to find out is… Could you back off a little?… You're not letting me think *[MARLEY takes a few steps back.]* What I want to know is… why does desire sometimes survive?… Or why… does it die?*[Pause.]*

MARLEY   That question… always pops up when desire is dying.   No sooner, no later.

IRIONDO   That's the most interesting thing that you have said so far! An intelligent thought here and there.] Well, thank goodness I waited. Maybe with you She learned the art of patience. And that was what made her…

MARLEY   I'm tired of this game.*[He moves as if he is going to leave, but he only takes a few steps. As if he did not know where to go.]*

IRIONDO   He's going to kill her, and that's no game.

MARLEY   She'll be fine. Even if it bothers us, She is at the beach with her husband.

IRIONDO   No, She's not fine. Not fine at all.

MARLEY   Why do you say that?

IRIONDO   ……

MARLEY   Quit playing hide-and-seek! If you have something to say, just say it! If not, shut up! I'm sick of you!

IRIONDO   Two days ago, She called me crying. He had threatened her again. This time he hit her. And when he had to leave the hotel, he left her with her hands and feet, tied to the bed. Then he cried and begged for forgiveness … he told her that the idea of losing her drove him mad. He'd never done anything like that before. She was very scared. What worries me is that She didn't call yesterday or today either.

MARLEY   Why didn't you tell me this before?

IRIONDO   I didn't trust you. I don't trust you now either, but…

MARLEY   You couldn't just say it?… You were aware of the danger and kept on playing… You sick coward! Why don't you tell me once and for all? *[MARLEY comes closer. He raises his fist. He is making a great effort to control himself. Slowly, he brings his fist closer to IRIONDO'S face.]* I hope nothing happens to her because…

IRIONDO	Because what?
MARLEY	Because I'll kill you! I'll kill you both! I'll kill the two of you!
IRIONDO	Swear it?
MARLEY	Yes, of course, I swear!
IRIONDO	You love her...
MARLEY	Madly!... And She loves me!... You better believe it!
IRIONDO	She doesn't...
MARLEY	Yes, She does!... She's going to leave her husband. She can't stand the situation any longer. The distance between us. Do you understand? Between us! She is going to leave everything for me. And I believe her. Did you hear?!... I believe her!
IRIONDO	She's not going to... leave me.
MARLEY	I promise you, She will. The community has come to an end.
IRIONDO	You... you tricked me. In the beginning, you acted indifferent, and I thought that perhaps I was mistaken.
MARLEY	About what?
IRIONDO	About everything, about everything I've done.
MARLEY	I don't trust you either, don't expect sincerity.
IRIONDO	I thought you were being quite sincere when you said you loved her madly.
MARLEY	Think what you will. Why don't you call her hotel?
IRIONDO	I don't know where they are. She's the one who calls me ... from pay phones.
MARLEY	We'll find her.
IRIONDO	And?
MARLEY	We can see how She's doing. If she needs anything.
IRIONDO	Are you going to rescue her?
MARLEY	I don't know, but I need to know that She's okay. *[Staring at him.]*

What's the matter? Weren't you banging you head against the wall, weren't you crying inconsolably? Didn't you feel mutilated?... And now that She's in danger...

IRIONDO   She's confused.

MARLEY   She's in danger!

IRIONDO   It's obvious... that She's very confused.

[Pause.]

MARLEY   Again the trap... you like to play...*[He pushes him furiously.]* Tell me! Tell me once and for all!

IRIONDO   I don't think you'll like it, but it's better that you find out as soon as possible.

MARLEY   Get to the point, you clown!

IRIONDO   Before leaving, She told me exactly the same thing... that She would leave everything for me. Everything.

MARLEY   That's a lie! You lie! You can't stand seeing yourself pushed aside! Defeated! You're making it up! You're delirious! Since you started talking, you haven't stopped lying and turning all this, into filth! Don't speak anymore, asshole! It's over!*[He walks towards an exit.]*

IRIONDO   Yes, it's over. He killed her. I know.

MARLEY   *[He stops.]* What do you know? How do you know?

IRIONDO   She would have called. For years She has called me everyday. Wherever She might be. It was her lucky charm. She had to do it. *"So everything will turn out okay."* She believes in these things. Nothing would have stopped her. Nothing. *[Pause.]*

He killed her. *[MARLEY collapses into the seat.]*

11.

[MARLEY is seated with his body hunched down. His hands are clasping his head. IRIONDO looks at him attentively for several minutes.]

IRIONDO   Are so many necessary... for desire to function? *[Pause.]* At first I followed you two... I was desperate with jealousy. I suffered a lot. Just the thought of what the two of you could be doing made me want to throw up, but... after seeing you many times, and noticing that nothing extraordinary happened between you... that both of you were always the same, that you didn't do anything crazy... you didn't run in the streets holding hands, laughing in the rain, like in the movies... people did not stop to look at you –people are very sensitive and curious about other people's happiness– but no, there was nothing special to bring on the lacerating venom of envy... Sometimes, I've even seen you, almost indifferent, serious, preoccupied. Staring at your shoes. Quiet. And when I got to see the two of you together, and could predict what you would do, I noticed that I would begin to get excited, yes, aroused by the situation... so I kept watching you, but now, for my own pleasure. Without knowing it, you two had become my biggest turn-on. That was when things got better with her. My sexual performance.

[MARLEY jumps on top of him. They wrestle falling to the floor. IRIONDO manages to grasp MARLEY'S throat and strangles him. MARLEY begins to suffocate. He tries desperately to get loose, but he can't. Finally, when he is about to collapse, IRIONDO releases him.]

IRIONDO   Did you have an erection?... or was it just my imagination? It always happens to hanged men. A purely physiological matter.

MARLEY   You almost... killed me.

IRIONDO   Yes, I don't know why I didn't.

MARLEY   You're not going to get her back this way.

IRIONDO   No.

MARLEY   She loves me.

IRIONDO   …….

MARLEY   I'm going to leave my wife.

IRIONDO   ….….

MARLEY   I don't sleep either. We've been preparing this for months.

IRIONDO   Shhh… be quiet. It's more than enough.*[Pause.]* I'm her husband.

MARLEY   ……

IRIONDO   I can't understand why didn't I kill you.

MARLEY   But, then… Where is She? Where is She? And… what was all that… that about how her husband had killed her? That he had hit her? *[He comes closer and starts shaking IRIONDO, who lets him.]* Answer me! Did you do something to her?… Where is She?… *[He slaps him.]* Where is She?!… Speak!… Where is She?! *[IRIONDO suddenly reacts and pushes him aside.]*

IRIONDO   We came back from the seashore. Yesterday. She's at home preparing her things. She's leaving.

MARLEY   Where to?!

IRIONDO   Calm down. With you… I guess. Weren't you organizing the escape?

MARLEY   That's why you put on this farce.

IRIONDO   I wanted to make sure I had done the right thing.

MARLEY   I never trusted you.

IRIONDO   You confessed many things. All the things I needed to know. And more. Much more than I wanted to know.

MARLEY   You lost. It's over. Leave her alone.

IRIONDO   Yes, that's the idea. Could you understand me if I told you that I wanted to know… and wanted to be mistaken? Yes, I did everything possible… yes, everything I could…

MARLEY   And the others? Do they exist?

IRIONDO   I told you, now it's your turn to get your hands dirty. *[Laughing.]* Fidelity…

MARLEY   What's the matter?

IRIONDO   I feel sorry for you.

MARLEY   Have you seen your face? You look dreadful.

IRIONDO   I can imagine you following her. Checking her calendar. Listening behind the doors.

MARLEY   I'd never even think of doing that.

IRIONDO   These things aren't thought, they're just done. They're impulses. Uncontrollable impulses. The terror of being left out takes you to unimaginable places… Shameful places. I don't want… to remember.

MARLEY   Do you still love her?

IRIONDO   Madly. *[Pause.]* The worst thing is… that it's something like… the feeling of being taken over.   That's the hardest thing of all. That everything points in the same direction. And leads time and time again, to what you want to forget. Her skin in my skin. Her eyes nailed to mine. My sex in hers. I… I who am no longer just myself. She inhabits me. She inhabits me.   Life, becomes a hideous commingling. A permanent dialogue with the impossible. A constant pinch. It is like having her name tattooed in each cell. At the tip of each nerve. It's… terrible. Unbearable.

MARLEY   Yes, I know what you're talking about.   *[Pause.]* I'm leaving.

IRIONDO   Yes, that would be best.

MARLEY   Don't think about following us.

IRIONDO   No. I promise.

MARLEY   And leave her alone. I wouldn't want to…

IRIONDO   What?

MARLEY   To have to get rid of you.

IRIONDO   Could you do it?

MARLEY   Yes.

IRIONDO   You love her. You truly love her.

MARLEY   Yes! Yes! How many times do I have to tell you?!

IRIONDO   Many, it would seem. It's good for me to hear it.

MARLEY   What are you saying?

IRIONDO   Everything is falling into place, it's all making sense.

MARLEY   She told me, *"He is mad. Totally insane."*

IRIONDO   Desperate. *[MARLEY starts to walk as if to leave.]* I hit her, I had never done it before. Her face, her body. She let me. She didn't resist. She didn't say a word. She seemed to enjoy it, to challenge me and find out how far I would go. I got furious. More. More still. My arm was moving mechanically. Coming and going. Fast. Out of control. There was just a scream...

MARLEY   What?... Are you saying?

IRIONDO   That you are not going to find her. He killed her.

MARLEY   No... no...

IRIONDO   She was packing her bags. Taking her things out of the bathroom cabinet. Her most intimate items. I saw the empty spaces in the drawers, the empty hangers... the house was turning into... paper. It was crumbling down. Nothing to lean on, nothing solid.

I stopped her before She could make it through the door.*[Pause.]*Now it's your turn to do the dirty work. You swore. I made you swear. You said, *"If something happens to her, I'll kill you."* Well...*[Pause.]*I've told you, I've told you several times... life without her... without her, I don't want it.

[IRIONDO and MARLEY are motionless. Facing each other. Staring at each other. Fists clenched. Faces and bodies in maximum tension. Their breathing becomes more and more agitated. Lights dim slowly to black. In the darkness,

only their amplified breathing can be heard, more and more intense. Then, total silence.]

Bibliography

Primary Sources:

Dueña y señora, Buenos Aires: Editorial La Campana, 1982.

Extraño juguete, Buenos Aires: Ediciones Búsqueda, 1987.

Y a otra cosa mariposa, Buenos Aires: Ediciones Búsqueda, 1988.

"Y a otra cosa mariposa," in *Voces en Escena Antología de Dramaturgas Latinoamericanas*, edited by Nora Eidelberg y María Mercedes Jaramillo. Medellín: Ed. Universidad de Antioquía, 1991.

"Nada entre los dientes," in *Monólogos de dos continents: Catorce textos teatrales de reconocidos autores españoles y argentinos*. Buenos Aires: Ed. Corregidor, 1999.

Una noche cualquiera. Sevilla: Edición del Area de Cultura del Ayuntamiento de Sevilla, 2000.

Desde los márgenes. Cuadernos Escénicos. Madrid: Casa de América, 2000.

"Cuerpos visibles/territorios sitiados," in *Escenografías del cuerpo: Actas del III Encuentro de Mujeres en las Artes Escénicas* (Cádiz, 1999), edited by Laura Borras Castanyer. Madrid: Ed. Fundación del Autor and S.G.A.E, 2000.

Secondary Sources:

Bauman, Kevin. "Metatexts, Women and Sexuality: The Facts and (PH) allacies in Torres Molina's *Extraño Juguete*." *Romance Languages Annual* 2 (1990): 330-35.

Bixler, Jaqueline E. "For Women only? The Theatre of Susana Torres Molina." *Latin American Women Dramatists: Theater, Texts, and Theories*. Eds. Catherine Larson and Margarita Vargas. Bloomington: Indiana University Press, 1998.

DiPucio, Denise. "Radical and Materialist Relationships in Torres Molina's *Extraño juguete*." *Letras Femeninas* vol. 21, 1-2 (Spring-Fall, 1995): 153-64.

Eidelberg, Nora. "Susana Torres Molina: destacada teatrista argentina." *Alba de America* 7- 12.13 (July 1989): 391-93.

Foster, David W. "Identidades polimórficas y planteo metateatral en *Extraño juguete* de Susana Torres Molina." *Alba de América* 7 – 12.13 (July 1989): 75-86.

Flores, Yolanda. *The Drama of Gender: Feminist Theatre by Women of the Americas*. Ann Arbor: Dissertation Abstracts International, 56-4 (Oct. 1995): 1378A.

Genovese, Gabriela. "Homoerotismo la resistencia cultural frente a la incomodidad patriarcal." Confluencia: Revista Hispánica de Literatura 15.2 (Spring 2000): 36-47.

Gladhart, Amalia. "Playing Gender." *Latin American Literary Review* 24-47 (Jan-June 1996): 59-89.

Green, Otis H. "Imaginative Authority in Spanish Literature." *PMLA: Publications of the Modern Language Association of America* 84 (1969): 209-216.

Jones, Jean Graham. "Myths, Masks, and Machismo: *Un trabajo fabuloso* by Ricardo Halac and *Y a otra cosa mariposa* by Susana Torres Molina." *Gestos: Teoría y práctica del teatro hispanico* 10-20 (November 1995): 91-106.

Seda, Laurietz. "El hábito no hace al monje: Travestismo, homosexualidad y lesbianismo en ... *y a otra cosa mariposa* de Susana Torres Molina." *Latin American Theatre Review* 30-2 (Spring 1997): 103-14.

Zayas de Lima, Perla. "Susana Torres Molina, la mujer y el mito." *Dramas de mujeres, libro sobre dramaturgas argentinas*. Buenos Aires: Editorial Ciudad Argentina, 1998.

---. "Tres metáforas sobre un país dominado." *Teatro argentino durante El Proceso (1976-1983)*, edited by Juana Arancibia and Zulema Mirkin. Buenos Aires: Editorial Vinciguerra, 1992.